The Art of Coarse Language

Spike Hughes

The Art of Coarse Language

Illustrated by *JOHN JENSEN*

Words, words, words.

SHAKESPEARE

HUTCHINSON OF LONDON

Hutchinson & Co (Publishers) Ltd
3 Fitzroy Square, London W1

London Melbourne Sydney Auckland
Wellington Johannesburg Cape Town
and agencies throughout the world

First published 1974
© Spike Hughes 1974
Illustrations © Hutchinson & Co (Publishers) Ltd 1974

Set in Monotype Baskerville
Printed in Great Britain by The Anchor Press Ltd
and bound by Wm Brendon & Son Ltd
both of Tiptree, Essex

ISBN 0 09 120040 7

TO CHARMIAN

whose speech is comely and — or rather, but —
whose spelling is a thing of beauty
and a joy for ever

Contents

1   *First Principles*

Language is the dress of thought

SAMUEL JOHNSON

Perhaps we should have felt honoured to find *The Art of Coarse Entertaining* reviewed in the *Times Literary Supplement* under the rubric 'Social Studies'; but we weren't. We weren't insulted, or even grateful. We just thought it was about time, too.

For if anything has been a Social Study for generations it is these books on the Coarse Arts. They are based entirely on what none of your modern social students, psychologists, statisticians, behaviourists or sociological prodnoses has ever known anything about: first-hand experience of the subject.

The present study is no exception to the tradition. And if anybody thinks that tradition is an outmoded idea – sorry, 'concept' – let them be reminded that we are dealing with a subject of such contemporaneousness, tricknowledgicality and universal meaningfulness that students take degrees in it: Communication.

By Communication they mean people talking to each other. For some reason this has become more important than it used to be, and apparently now needs researching into. It is difficult to see why, since the world seems to be crammed to explosion point with people talking to each

other with no trouble at all – interminably, all at once and whether they have anything to say or not. Like disc jockeys and town councillors.

Coarse Language is the simplest form of Communication, and is based on the principle that while one word should be used in preference to three, there are times when three short words are better used than one long one – a practice which not only leads to better English, but to increased financial reward for journalists who are paid by the word.

We may not all be born Coarse cricketers, cooks, gardeners, bridge players or hosts, for it is possible for some under-privileged people to go through life with neither talent nor time for any of these arts; but unless deprived of speech by some natural misfortune we are all of us speakers of Coarse Language when we first begin to talk as babies.

This is the use of Coarse Language in its most natural form, where grammar, syntax and pronunciation play no part, but an inflexion, a grimace or a simple gesture can make the same simple word serve as a statement, a question, a plea, a refusal or a demand.

Unfortunately, this innocent form of communication is soon defiled by the evil influence of parents, who suddenly decide that their child is half-witted and must be taught baby-talk. Baby-talk is a very useful language, but not to babies – unless they intend to be journalists or PROs or ad. men when they grow up. Then they will find it invaluable in describing public figures by such coy names as 'Mr Europe', 'Mr Football', 'Mr Channel Tunnel' or 'Mr Down-Under', and inventing nursery cutenesses like zebra crossings and panda cars, and the pinta (what is the plural of that – pintas?).

Parents, indeed, are a child's worst handicap. He would be perfectly happy learning to speak if he didn't have to speak to his parents and other idiots like them. No sooner has he learnt simple monosyllables like cow, cat, dog, duck, pot, horse, train, car, lamb or sheep, than he finds he has to embellish them in order to make himself understood by grown-ups who talk about moo-cows, pussy-cats (why not mew-cats?), doggies and bow-wows, quack-quacks, potties, gee-gees, puff-puffs, car-cars and baa-lambs. (As grown-ups apparently cannot pronounce sheep *they* have to be called baa-lambs too.)

These infantilisms become increasingly unintelligible to babies anyway. With pasture land being sold to specu-lators so fast that in ten years' time milk will have to be imported to feed the people who live in the 'develop-ment', children now scarcely know what a cow is, let alone that it moos. Or that the hypertrophied deep-frozen mass that passes for lamb nowadays can ever have baa'd in its over-fed life.

'Puff-puff' is hopelessly out of date, but still used for

train. I expect it is too much to hope for that it has been replaced by anything as comparably apt as 'stink-stink' for a diesel engine.

Again, unless he is a regular race-goer, there is no reason for a baby to think that a 'gee-gee' is a horse (and if he *did* go to the races he would know better than ever that the 'gee-gees' that carried his money are not horses but dormice). Certainly few modern children can ever have heard a coachman or rag-and-bone man saying 'gee-up' to his nag.

The infliction of a vocabulary of baby-talk on the beginner is unforgivably against the very essence of Coarse Language. It is unnecessarily elaborate, retards the child's progress in the proper use of English, and has to be laboriously unlearnt.

The process of unlearning takes place at school, when the fanciful prefixes of baby-talk are replaced by the austerity of abbreviations that can reduce the English language to a code which outsiders cannot understand. Nouns and adjectives consist of single, incomplete syllables of the original words and make the Neapolitan dialect sound verbose in comparison.

The staccato, and generally monosyllabic, language of schoolboys varies, not from generation to generation, but virtually from term to term. Whether they have been in constant use from the time I left school until today, I don't know; but there are nevertheless certain words which still seem to be timeless. A prefect is still a 'pre', things are 'supe' or 'fab', 'wiz' or 'terrif' or a 'swizz'; you still hope for 'congrats' if your exploits get a 'mensh' in the school 'mag'.

Like baby-talk, school-talk needs unlearning; and a tough business that can be, for once you've been bitten by the bug of abbreviation you take a lot of verbal delousing to get back to the simple joys and beauties of true Coarse Language.

The unlearning of school-talk does not mean, of course, that the well-chosen abbreviation is not used in later life. The fluent speaker of rhyming slang always omits the actual rhymes from his phrases, and as a result it is permissible to describe a stupid man as a berk, a woman as a Jane, and to give somebody a raspberry in respectable company. Indeed, there are prim people going around who talk of a 'raspberry' and a 'berk' who would die of shame if they knew how the expressions were derived.

For those of us who know their meaning they form a convenient secret language that can be spoken in any company with little chance of the uninitiated recognizing them as – to use the lexicographer's own familiar abbreviation – 'vulg.'

Abbreviations abound in professional jargon, and so do traps for the unpractised layman who wants to join in. For years, for instance, the music critics of *The Times*, to show their erudition, have talked about jazz 'breaks'. There is such a thing as a 'break' of course, but what *The Times* was hearing was a solo chorus, which is something quite different.

On the other hand, where journalists often get other people's jargon wrong, they themselves suffer almost physical pain when those other people can't get everyday newspaper terms right – like saying 'article' instead of 'story' or 'piece', 'para' instead of 'par', or 'advert' instead of 'ad.'

The most dangerous period in the life of the student of Coarse Language is the transition from adolescent to adult. Schoolboy slang has to be forgotten and replaced by a language that conforms to the principles of the Art.

The natural reaction to monosyllabic abbreviations is to go to the other extreme and affect a high-sounding, pedantic and pompous vocabulary in order to appear grown-up.

The student must nevertheless learn this exaggerated vocabulary carefully for two reasons: to know what not to say, and to understand what other people mean when they use it.

The use of inflated, would-be refined language, as distinct from the coarse variety the rest of us speak, is the result of a belief by shopkeepers, bank managers, tax inspectors, local government officers, businessmen, advertising agents, journalists, politicians, lawyers, civil servants, judges, B.Sc.'s, economists, BBC reporters, trade union leaders, tycoons, insurance brokers, estate agents, policemen, sociologists, educationalists, clergymen, psychologists, antique dealers, motor salesmen, travel agents, art critics, film critics, financial correspondents, writers on wine, book reviewers and Whitehall spokesmen, that they are in some way superior beings (from whom Good Lord deliver us), and so must use superior language.

It is difficult to talk and otherwise communicate with these ethnic groups because, unless you use the language they speak, they do not consider you serious. It is no good telling an inquisitive policeman that you are going to see a man about a dog. You have to be proceeding to consult a person in a matter appertaining to a dog. For all their mobile units and VHF radio links, the Force still plods through the English language with the dignified tread of the man on the beat.

Similarly, you must not expect rapid service from a commercial firm if you write to them saying: 'Thank you for your letter. I enclose a cheque.' It will take them some time to work out that what you mean is that you are in receipt of their communication of the 31st inst., the contents of which you have duly noted, and accordingly please will they find cheque in payment of the goods, and a lot more of etc., etc.

In cases where specialist jargon gets too much for your patience (and the jargon of commercial letter-writers is one of the worst for this), the use of invented language in letters to sales managers and their kind can soothe the nerves and be quietly enjoyable:

'Dear Sir,' you write, 'With referral to your letter in respondment to my request for detailability data concerning the goods in question, I envoyize herewith cheque in settlance.

'In termination may I ask you to please maxpedite despatch transportationwise . . .'

A letter like this will greatly impress the recipient and probably inspire him to add your neologisms to his own pompous vocabulary. People who believe that escalation is a real word and that 'hopefully' means 'it is hoped', will believe every word you write.

The style and extent of invented language vary, of course, with each situation. Some inventions are best spoken, some are more effective when they are written. Some invented phrases are peculiar to a single family (there are few families without their own idiom), and while they may be used in the presence of strangers they very rarely achieve more than a limited circulation. This is a pity, for many of them are extremely expressive and versatile and would be a considerable adornment to everyday English.

In our family we have the word 'ugh'. This is derived from the familiar expression of revulsion used by characters in comics, 'Ugh!' It is pronounced 'ugg', however, this being my nephew Robin's reading of the word on first

seeing it in print as a small boy. As an adjective it means revolting, drab, unpretty, unattractive, boring, commonplace, unpleasant, and just plain nauseating. To 'feel ugh' means to feel unwell.

As a transitive verb 'to ugh', together with the highly idiomatic use of the adjective in 'to be ugh to [person]', means to assert authority, to discipline, to scold, to nag, to be beastly – depending on whether you are the ugher or the ughee.

2 *How to Earn a Living*

Doers of the word, and not hearers

EPISTLE OF JAMES, I. 22

Coarse Language, at its best, is easily intelligible, direct and simple. It is the language which you and I speak and write to each other and our friends. Unfortunately, unless we use it with the skill and imagination of Winston Churchill or Bernard Shaw we are not likely to make a fortune out of it. The best it can do for us is to save us the trouble of switching into 'commercialese' in order to write business letters like other business-letter-writers.

But even this can't be guaranteed to earn us a living. We have to stoop to conquer and adapt (some might say prostitute) ourselves to the peculiar forms of mutilated, and often improperly learnt, English of whatever profession, trade, business, art, craft or racket we may be forced to follow in order to eat.

Today – I mean, at this moment in time – the career with the really endless opportunities for the skilled linguist with an ear for the currently fashionable cadences and twists of the English language, is that of a BBC reporter, announcer, newsreader, or even hired speaker.

No awkward qualifications are asked for beyond a university degree. This is essential, however, as a guarantee that you will not be handicapped by education in a

profession where the smallest grain of learning is a dangerous thing. (The great illusion of employers since the War
is that a degree is in some way a proof of education. It is
nothing of the sort, of course; it is a proof of being able to
pass examinations, which is another matter altogether.)

Proficiency as a modern BBC broadcaster is a question
of training in two basic skills: imitation of the prevailing
manner of broadcasting, and a sure touch in mispronouncing and putting the wrong stresses on English words.

The mis-stressing, or at least unconventional stressing,
of English is favoured by so many broadcasters because,
like the members of the many other trades and professions
I listed in the last chapter, they imagine that they are
something special, and should therefore spice up their
pronunciation with a touch of what they think is American
usage. This is to make it all sound contemporary and
meaningful.

Unfortunately, what the ambitious broadcaster thinks is
American usage often turns out to be a mis-stressing of a
word which has the same accentuation in both English
and American.

An announcer on Radio 4 was heard to talk of 'aggran-
*dize*ment', not knowing that though the Americans may
pronounce the 'ize' to rhyme with 'eyes', they nevertheless still stress the second syllable as we do (or thought we
did). With this mid-Atlantic contortion of aggrandizement
the speaker obviously aimed to appear well-travelled and
sophisticated, and may well have kidded some of his
listeners into believing he was. But surely not for long,
for in virtually the same breath he referred to Franklin
Roosevelt as 'Ruse-velt', thus showing that he was neither
well-travelled nor sophisticated, but just very 'O' level
modern BBC, after all.

BBC 'O' level English is renowned for its liberal

19

approach to the language, which enables the broadcaster to stress, pronounce and construct words in an entirely individual manner. The manner is not so individual, however, that the foreigner cannot understand it. Indeed, as the public practice of pronouncing English as it is spelt increases, so it is easier for the foreigner to recognize words he has read, but has never been able to understand when spoken. Or at least, it should be easier.

Unfortunately, different announcers have different ways of mispronouncing the same word, and so confuse both the native and the foreign listener. Only last week a Radio 4 announcer told us to make a point of listening to a Mr 'Hooston' – obviously Renée Houston's brother, I thought. But apparently not, for a couple of days later another announcer's trailer referred to a Mr 'Husston'. It was only when Roy Plomley finally addressed his guest in 'Desert Island Discs' as Mr 'Hewston' that I discovered they'd been trying all along to tell us about John Huston.

No hard-and-fast rules there, you'll note. This may be the result of a BBC policy of permissiveness which does not like to interfere with the rights of the citizen to treat the English language with violence and obscenity.

Or (more likely) it is the result of the ignorance of the authorities, who are capable of presenting a speaker in the Third Programme to talk about music and don't see anything odd in his reference to his 'enthusi-isms'.

However, we must all respect each other's right to Free Speech and not wince too noticeably when a BBC commentator describes the Press as 'laskivious', a newsreader refers to a 'cykerlist' and Can*berra*, or demonstrates yet again that he doesn't know how to distinguish words like 'increase' and 'survey' used as nouns from the same words used as verbs.

He is just as shaky – or as fabulously sophisticated – with the word 'dispute', which he now *acc*ents in the American manner and so makes it impossible for Cowper's famous lines to scan:

> I am monarch of all I *sur*vey,
> My right there is none to *dis*pute;

And just to show you that when the stress on the first syllable would be correct, he will tell you that the whole affair is highly dis*put*able, and kindly don't be so ob-*du*rate.

The Third Programme (they may call it Radio 3, but it's still the Third Programme to me), provides particularly happy opportunities for the 'O' level English speaker who also fancies himself as a speaker of low-level French.

The Third Programme is famous for its encouragement of critics and arts experts who have caht blontch to air their opinions on the day-corps (as opposed to the night-corps) of the latest ballet or Vurdi opera at Covent Garden, to talk of the Debewssy on-sombull, and the tendency of modern novelists to suffer from the Malays found in all decadent literature.

In fact, so much abuse is directed against the Malays we are all said to suffer from, that one wonders whether it isn't time the matter was taken up by the Race Relations Board.

Another word much fancied by those who have passed low-level French (and almost as popular as Humphrey Lyttelton's favourite, the gawmay) is the word pronounced *repawtahj*. This is particular fun for the Coarse Linguist, because though the French use it, the word is in fact English.

The French have no word of their own for a newspaper reporter; they use ours, and to describe what a reporter does, concoct the term *reportage*, which is the same as the rather ungainly English 'reportage'. To avoid ungainliness and acquire a little *chic* the critics, arts reporters and other *savants* pronounce reportage as though it were French, and therefore a cut above the obvious, but rather unglamorous, word, reporting.

(In France a credit is given on television to the man in charge of mixing the sound. They call it *mixage*. Why haven't we heard that word here yet? Or are the arts boys losing their touch?)

Where the Red Queen told Alice to speak in French when she couldn't think of the English for a thing, the Coarse Linguist who wishes to shine in modern intellectual company will speak French when he *can* think of the English for a thing.

This practice is a firmly established form of snobbery, and if you can't think of a French word where a perfectly good English one would do, you simply use an entirely made-up or unidiomatic French word, content in the knowledge that it will not be questioned by your audience, because they will never admit they don't understand French, even yours.

You can quite safely talk about the BBC *annoncière* you heard; it is, after all, a genuine French word. You can use it safely because nobody present will know that the French for a girl announcer is a *speakerine,* and that an *annoncière* is a woman who looks after the small ads in a French newspaper.

If, so far, we have been concerned with the prospects of a BBC career with the Third Programme and Radio 4 only, it is because the language used on Radios 1 and 2 is so simple as to be virtually unintelligible. What little one can understand (and this goes for BBC local radio as well) is on the level of the market place and the doorstep commercial traveller. Not surprisingly, really, considering that the object of this sort of communication is to try to sell as much mediocrity as possible.

This is done by greeting the audience with 'Ladies!' ('I know you ladies will dig this next record'), and the telling of appallingly elementary funny stories which all end in giggles because the teller gives the point away prematurely.

The language of disc jockeys and local radio news-readers is like that heard in the Open University broadcasts – a private language understood only by fully paid-up members. Not that private languages are without interest to the outsider. There is an undeniable fascination in listening to *teachers* who tell their pupils that the 's'lution' to a problem is to '*dis*tribute' the factors, refer to 'normative aspects', use 'notion' for 'idea', and in the course of 'methodological conclusions' announce that 'man is a maximizing animal'.

There is no doubt that language like this has a certain exotic charm – rather like Sanskrit; but it is beyond the scope of Coarse Language, which is universally understood, if not (for reasons we have seen) universally appreciated, and is a living contradiction of Voltaire's assertion that people 'only use words to disguise their thoughts'.

3 'A Rhapsody of Words'

Though you and I may pride ourselves on being living contradictions of Voltaire's tag, we are still faced with the problem of living with those whose life is passed almost entirely in using words to disguise their thoughts.

These unfortunates – the rhapsodists of Shakespeare's phrase – suffer from the chronic and highly infectious complaint known as the euphemisms. It is not only infectious; it is injected into the young as a form of immunization against Coarse Language which – I am sorry to say – is often partially successful.

There can be few of us who are not haughty about people who refer to 'the toilet' instead of the lavatory, even though we know perfectly well that lavatory is already a euphemism. To those in what is known (euphemistically) as the lower income bracket, toilet is obviously more refined and respectable than lavatory, which they somehow consider blunt and rather crude. But whereas we know the literal meaning of lavatory, as a place to wash in, they are inevitably surprised when they first encounter the word toilet used in its original sense.

After a childhood of the word meaning only one thing, they suddenly read in a novel that Lady Caroline was discovered at her toilet. This always leads to giggles and causes much confusion in the young mind when it is faced with displays in shops of toilet soap, toilet preparations, toilet accessories, and God-knows-how-many other 'toilet-eries'. Ambiguity is added to euphemism.

Today the English euphemism is at an interesting stage in its history. As few subjects are regarded as taboo any longer, the need for euphemisms grows less urgent.

This latest development should make life much easier for us who have always tried to avoid using euphemisms, and have spent a lifetime trying to discover what other people's mean.

Or so one might think.

In fact, what has happened is that the original words and phrases which demanded euphemisms are now used without embarrassment in polite conversation, schools

broadcasts and the public Press, and have become euphemisms themselves – for the old four-letter (vulg.) words. As society changes so the present taboo on vulg. words will disappear and they in turn will become euphemisms for a new set of expressions borrowed from the Yiddish (a particularly rich territory), French, German and Italian.

Gaelic, too, might help, since knuckle-rapping critics think one is resorting to slang whenever one uses English words deriving from perfectly proper non-slang Gaelic. I was once reproached by a reviewer for being 'too chatty and colloquial' in using the word 'cock-eyed' in a history of Glyndebourne. The word comes from the respectable Gaelic word *caog*, to wink, to take aim by shutting one eye; a *caogshuil* is a squint eye.

I should have known, of course. A squint is rather vulgar; one talks of people having a 'cast' in the eye. The right word to describe the situation would have been 'strabismic'.

Though not yet qualifying as a Senior Citizen, I nevertheless enjoy what is known as presbyopia – a form of long-sightedness incident to old age. This not only enables me to read a car number-plate at two feet, with glasses if worn, but to remember a time, not so very long ago, when euphemisms were even more ridiculous than today.

In those revolutionary 1920s, for instance, when women of thirty had at last been given the vote, when Stravinsky was 'cacophony', when the Jazz Age was in full swing and had nothing whatever to do with jazz, the imminent birth of the present Lord Harewood was proclaimed on newspaper display bills with the words 'Accouchement of Princess Mary'.

Just as today the subject of death and dying is still

avoided in conversation and in print by saying that someone has passed away, passed over, passed on, and – in local papers – been called to rest or even gone to Jesus; and lawyers refer to somebody as being deceased instead of dead (granted it's cheaper to cable 'the deceased' than 'the dead man'), so in my youth nobody could bring themselves to say that a woman was pregnant, or going to have a baby.

The most daring description was that she was an expectant mother. Otherwise she was awaiting a happy event, in an interesting condition, a certain condition (if she was found murdered), or – in educated company – *enceinte*.

Very oo-la-la to use French, of course. But so far from being riskay and near the *je ne sais quoi*, the final genteelness of using French as camouflage for calling a pregnancy a pregnancy, the phrase *enceinte* was itself a euphemism.

The term (which also means ramparts) was defined in a famous French dictionary of the time as 'se dit d'une femme grosse', which could be misleadingly translated as 'says itself of a gross woman'; but that would be *une grosse femme*. A *femme grosse* is a pregnant woman, and rather crudely put at that.

Today's edition of the same famous dictionary now tells us that *enceinte* 'se dit d'une femme qui porte un enfant dans son sein' – which we recognize, of course, as saying itself 'of a woman who carries a child in her . . .' But wait a minute. *Sein* is breast or bosom, or lap. It is also understood by the French to mean womb, other synonyms being *matrice* or matrix, and *flancs* – which also means flanks, sides, breasts, bosoms, entrails and bowels. *Tu paies ton argent, et tu prends ton choix . . .*

In spite of the present fashion for calling a prostitute a whore, instead (owing to the Street Offences Act) of a street-walker, much was recently heard of call-girls. The term was indignantly derided in Parliament and other public wash-tubs as a euphemism.

Maybe it is. But it is also an important trade description, which distinguishes one class of trollop from the rest. Patronizing a call-girl is like being a private patient: you make an appointment instead of waiting about with the rest of the mob.

If 'call-girl' was regarded by some as a euphemism, it led to a rash of dysphemisms in the Press, and there were the inevitable lurid headlines telling us of VICE IN-QUIRIES. The only vice in the whole affair was the one in which the Press, but not the public, was held by an unusually tame scandal for the time of day.

One of the purposes of the euphemism as a verbal device, I suppose, is to deceive. It is the old-school-tie of the hypocrite. Its power to deceive grows less and less every day, with one notable exception: the idea that The Lower Income Bracket is a euphemism for the working classes.

This is believed by almost everybody, particularly car-workers. It is not believed by those who recognize it as a dead straight literal description of their own circumstances. The true Lower Income Bracket is where the ageing educated middle classes, old scholars and writers, schoolmasters and retired nurses, and all who are trying to live on tiny fixed incomes, are found.

I fear, however, that the present decline of the euphemism promises no more than a false dawn. Already there are signs of revival encouraged, I am sorry to say, by one of Her Majesty's judges.

Some years ago the President of the Probate, Divorce and Admiralty Division had strong words to say on the reprehensible habit of talking about 'misconduct' and 'intimacy', instead of adultery – which is after all what the Seventh Commandment tells thee thou shalt not commit.

Now, alas, the English puritan spirit seems to be rising again, and sexual intercourse is no longer permissible – the phrase, I mean. As though embarrassed to use such a straightforward description of the straightforward act he was talking about, the judge in a recent rape case referred to the victim's having 'had sex'. Perhaps because it was shorter, he felt 'having sex' was cosier, less formal – more like having a smoke.

On the other hand, abbreviation is a recognized form of euphemism designed mainly to hide the speaker's embarrassment – VD, GPI, DTs, Moss Bros, for instance.

The danger of the euphemistic abbreviation like 'having sex', however, is that the word sex will come to mean only one thing – just as 'toilet' now has for half the population. Harmless clichés like 'the fair sex', or official forms that ask the sex of the filler-up, will be greeted with giggles or ribaldry, or such shocked indignation that such things should be mentioned, let alone asked, by the authorities, that there will be massed demonstrations in Trafalgar Square by the SPCK – the Society for the Prevention of Carnal Knowledge.

While the future of the euphemism as a means of hiding embarrassment and keeping taboo subjects at arm's length may be a little uncertain, the continued use of the euphemism to deceive, to make things sound better and grander than they really are, seems fairly well assured. Not just assured, but an indispensable part of the policy and vocabulary of local government officials and planners.

For centuries a small road in our village has been known as Church Lane; it leads from the main road to the church.

But the name was obviously too direct and informative, so it has now been changed by some body or other to the genteel Vicarage Way.

This has been put up, at the ratepayers' expense, on a sign that looks as though it had been given away with a packet of seeds, and is entirely in keeping with the prevailing ambition of modern rural authorities to better themselves, and to live, if not with all the amenities of the town, at least with the ready-mix graciousness and refinement of the garden suburb.

As a result of recent 'developments' in the village, there is now a proliferation, not of lanes or roads any more, but of Ways, Avenues and Drives, and desirable plastic reminders of a rural past like Foxglove Close, Mill Mead and – as urban ambition, but not urbanity, encroaches – a Crescent, probably the first in any English village.

The new residents are naturally delighted by such elegance and cut-glass classiness; even one of the older villagers was heard to regret that she still lived in a road. However, she was proud, in fact rather stuck up, that her son lived in 'a very good class of neighbourhood' in South London, with an address in Tulip Avenue.

On the other hand, try as the Post Office may to get the inhabitants to number their houses and use a postal code, nothing will prevent an Englishman naming his castle according to his fancy.

The Avenues, Drives, Meads, Closes, Ways, Crescents are filled with desirable residences bearing comforting names (and I read from the electoral register) like Dunromin, None Snugger, Kozikot, and Pax Vobiscum; evocative nostalgic names like Grinzing, Stresa, Lugano, Kandersteg, Montana, Avalon; sad names like Minnow End; cute names like Nought, Hi-Tymes, Jonjo and Pegasus; puzzling names like Dun-i (etym. dub.? perhaps from 'I dunnit, dun I?'), and Patterns.

The most intriguing name, however, and one which is resolutely non-conformist in both rural and garden-suburb surroundings, is that of Tishomingo. I can only imagine that this was inspired by a love for a famous Duke Ellington record of the 1920s called *Tishomingo Blues*.

In fairness it should be remembered that the French can be every bit as awful as the English in naming their bungalows and chalets. Though most people imagine it is a purely English conceit, there are in fact almost as many houses named Mon Repos in France as there are in England.

The French, too, are every bit as capable of cuteness as we are, and produce champion examples like Sam Suffit – *ça me suffit* – which is an almost exact equivalent of a bungalow seen in Scotland called Thistledoo.

And, of course, the French can be as soppy as anyone. I once stayed in a villa near Nice called Sonjadou – which is Provençal for Sweet Dream (*songe doux*). When I last saw it the name had been changed to Villa Jenkins. That was overdoing no-nonsense-about-us a bit, I thought.

4   *Humpdumptism*

*'When I use a word,' Humpty Dumpty said in
rather a scornful tone, 'it means just what I
choose it to mean – neither more nor less.'*

THROUGH THE LOOKING-GLASS

The delight in the euphemism found in so many spheres of
English, and particularly public, life is matched by the
obsessive preoccupation of the British Press with the
synonym.

Where the euphemism is used to avoid words or phrases
that embarrass the speaker or might shock the listener,
the synonym is used in Fleet Street to avoid the ordinary,
everyday word that first comes into the English head. It is a
display of sophistication, designed to impress the reader
with the writer's erudition and university background.

It is also, as often as not, a display of the writer's near-
literacy – not only of the writer but of the editors who
allow these frequent solecisms to get into print. How,
otherwise, can we explain such phrases as 'Mr Callaghan
will telegram . . .', or 'the decision to revaluate . . .', or
'it is almost doubtless that he will . . .'?

It is almost doubtless that the authors were convinced
they had found neat new synonyms for 'telegraph',
'revalue' and 'certain'; but it is typical that the second of
them doesn't exist, and the other two are used illiterately.

Now, these junketings with the English language are
not from what might be called the wilder shores of

34

journalism. They are taken from *The Times* which, like its contemporaries the *Sunday Times* and the *Daily Telegraph,* is a constant and fruitful source of unconscious neologisms and novel solecisms, and well worth studying by the Coarse Linguist who has a newspaper career in mind.

There may, of course, prove to be rather more competition than you might think. Few of us, I mean, can produce sentences like this one from a Quality television critic: 'Fred Trueman . . . attacks the commentary like it was the opening overs in a Roses match.'

On the other hand, once you get the hang of things you can let your imagination have its head, and no questions asked. With practice you can create little gems like chickens being 'defeathered', or somebody claiming 'descendance' from a noble family (both in the *Daily Telegraph*).

For those who have ambitions to write a gossip column the Quality columnists are a model for all who wish to succeed in this form of journalism. They are most inventive, and rarely at a loss for a good synonym. There was the spectacular introduction, for instance, of 'polylingual' into the English language by the *Sunday Times*. It not only made a change from the outmoded 'multiglot', but also showed that the author knew *two* dead languages and was well on the way to creating a third.

In addition to its columnists the Quality Press has plenty of space in which specialist contributors can spread their jargon and vogue words – arts critics, economists, city editors, fashion writers and other gossips. It is in these ranks that the Coarse Linguist may find a profitable career, for he starts with the advantage of already knowing the right and obvious words for things, and so knowing what *not* to say.

Arts criticism is probably the sphere where least knowledge of the English language – or at any rate, of its correct usage – is required This is because the arts are foreign and not altogether respectable, and so have to be discussed with liberal use of foreign words, in order to disguise the horrors of the truth – and, particularly, to display the writer's erudition and suggest his superior status.

Thus there is a generation of critics brought up to talk of an artist's *œuvre* without apparently knowing that there are two ordinary English words for what they're discussing – work and output. In any case, why must the

word be French? What is the matter with the German *Werk* or the Italian *opera*?

However, there does seem to be a faint chance that *œuvre* is going to be given a rest. A reviewer in the *Sunday Times* recently referred to Vladimir Nabokov's 'opus', so we can reasonably expect the lead to be followed by Fleet Street's huge corps of intellectual copycats. (It goes without saying that few of these critics ever go to France; otherwise they would know that the smarter French writers now refer to an artist *et son output*.)

That *Sunday Times* reviewer's inspired use of opus will certainly be hailed as a great find among the jetsam of criticism – except, of course, that it will be described as a *trouvaille*, to make it more literary.

One of the principal difficulties facing both critics and columnists is to distinguish between historic and historical, classic and classical, economic and economical.

The humblest punter would never refer to the Derby as a classical race, for instance, nor a modest author writing a history of England describe his study as historic. But a music critic cheerfully told us how much he admired 'Sir Adrian Boult's economic gestures'.

The picture suggested by this has its charm, to be sure; one sees the conductor handing out lavish Christmas bonuses to his orchestra. But that isn't at all what the critic meant. (It was also a music critic who produced one of my all-time favourite euphemisms in describing Tito Gobbi as having 'a tendency to cling to the upper side of the note' – in other words, to sing sharp.)

If knowing what people mean when they use a euphemism is difficult, it is not nearly so hard as translating the brand of English used with such bland assurance by the Quality Press.

I am not sure who is top of this particular league, but

the *Sunday Times* and its Atticus column keep up a very high standard of gibberish. The words themselves are not gibberish, but they are so misunderstood by the writer that they are nonsense to the educated reader.

After his gift of 'polylingual' to a grateful nation, Atticus produced a paragraph which must rate as a classic: 'Greeks say that forgetfulness of old friends is not one of their many defects . . .'

It took some time to work out that it was not the old friends who were not forgetful, but the Greeks.

Now that The Media – or as we say in English, Press and broadcasters – have accepted the American mistranslation of the German word *hoffentlich* ('it is to be hoped') as 'hopefully' (which in German would be *hoffnungsvoll*, or 'full of hope'), it is almost impossible to use the word correctly any more. Even some of one's best friends, who ought to know better, have caught the disease and presume you can only mean what they now mean when, hopefully, you use the word as P. G. Wodehouse and other old fuddle-duddles use it.

Meanwhile, the careless use of hopefully continues to make idiotic reading and we get the fatuous statement that 'Hopefully, the Treasury will reduce the tax . . .'

Once having got the taste for the grotesque misuse of hopefully it was not long before Fleet Street turned its attention to other adverbs which we previously thought had only one possible meaning.

The first word to get the treatment was 'thankfully'. A cricket columnist in the *Sunday Times,* well up in the table as usual, wrote: 'Thankfully, the ball went wide.' A grateful cricket ball is a bit of whimsy that not even cricket writers have thought of before. One supposes he meant luckily or fortunately. The trouble is one can't be sure.

Naturally, it didn't take long for thankfully to turn up wrongly used in the Top People's Top Paper Top Travel article.

Not that *The Times* can't think up novelties like this for itself. A few weeks later we read in its columns: 'Regretfully, the German traveller seems to be as firmly attached to his car as the Briton . . .' Is the German traveller regretful? Could be; but it doesn't make much sense. Perhaps 'regrettably' was too un-toply commonplace.

This is obviously a game that can be played indefinitely. Let us look at that first sentence again: 'Hopefully, the Treasury will reduce the tax . . .' Loosely translated, hopefully can mean 'we hope'. If one's information on the subject is a bit more definite then one can risk saying 'we think', instead of 'we hope'. But as we don't want to say so in common words of one syllable we now write: 'Thoughtfully, the Treasury will reduce the tax . . .'

And from there we can go to 'Regretfully, the Treasury will not reduce the tax . . .' (which is a lie if ever there was one); and 'Eagerly [we are eager that], the Treasury should reduce the tax . . .'; and 'Sorrowfully [we are sorry that], the Treasury will not reduce the tax . . .', and so on with 'suggestively', 'expectantly' or 'wishfully'.

There is one adverb, however, which cannot be used in this modish way: the word 'temporarily'. We cannot say 'Temporarily, the Treasury will reduce the tax . . .' because in Whitehall temporarily doesn't mean 'for the time being'. It means permanently. Like Purchase Tax which was introduced as a temporary measure to cut down spending during the 1939-45 war. It lasted temporarily for a good thirty years, until April 1973, when it was continued under the guise of VAT.

Like the adverb, the preposition has come in for a pretty rough time in the Quality Press of Fleet Street, and for the same reason: ignorance of the meaning of words apparently used because they look nice, and which the writer hopes will mean what he wants them to.

One of the most commonly misused prepositions seems to be 'for'. The solemn assertion by a gossip columnist that a friend had a phobia for Russian music, at once made one wonder whether the writer didn't perhaps mean mania. The context didn't help much either way. If the writer knew that phobia meant fear, did he mean that his friend feared for Russian music? If he meant that he was afraid of it then he could have said so quite simply in English anyway, without having to drag in a lot of Greek.

Once you start having trouble with your prepositions, of course, ambiguity sets in. Our columnist, on his record, would obviously define agoraphobia as a fear for open spaces, a feeling deeply shared by all who have the environment at heart, and may therefore rank as agoramaniacs. This makes agoraphobia mean two entirely opposite things – as neat a verbal trick as Fleet Street ever thought up.

We are now, as you will see, in deepest Looking-Glass Land, EC4, where Humpty Dumpty not only writes for the Quality papers, but owns them. There is the authentic Humpty Dumpty touch of genius in the muddle of verb, noun and preposition in the now familiar confession made – usually on the air – by enthusiastic admirers of the the arts that they 'have a fascination for Liza Minnelli'.

To which one can only retort that that, surely, was for Miss Minnelli to say, not the speaker. It's only by looking in the looking-glass that you can see what they mean. To you and me, the comprehension of words as they are used by other people is now in effect a double process and takes twice as long as it used to. (I am sorry to say that the habit of having a fascination for, instead of being fascinated by, seems to be very catching, and that it has even infected – twice – an expert wordsman like Roy Plomley in his 'Desert Island Discs'.)

41

The Coarse Linguist, proficient in Humpdumptism, is nevertheless likely to be bewildered, not by the writers' cavalier treatment of meaning (which is permitted by the rules of Humpdumptism), but by their quite remarkable ignorance of the most elementary grammatical function of the preposition.

In the *Daily Telegraph* we read: 'The Federation, like the farmers, attributed Press publicity for the fall in prices . . .' If attributed now means the same as blamed I can foresee some intriguing abuse and counterabuse when it is a question of whether an Old Master should be attributed by one lot of experts to Leonardo, or blamed on him by another.

(In *The Times* they have so much trouble with prepositions that they find themselves using conjunctions instead: 'Discerning wine drinkers will prefer a good Italian or other French wine than [*sic*] a bottle of Château Montrose at £10 a bottle . . .')

The solecism of 'phobia for' might be excused on the grounds that phobia is a foreign word and is likely to remain so to those who have suffered English mass-education. But when the preposition is wrongly used with the wrong word (as in 'fascination for' and, recently, 'fascination at'), and guessing what the speaker means becomes a toss-up, then it is time a fool-proof, all-purpose preposition was adopted for the convenience of Fleet Street columnists, reporters and headline writers, and all who speak by, with, from, in, on, at and through the television and radio.

To a certain extent this is already happening. The word 'on' in news headings is increasingly used as a convenient substitute (because it consists of only two letters instead of four) for 'over' – 'Row On Maplin', 'Britain Relents On Site for EEC Fund', 'Wilson Rebuke On Firms'.

There is no great ambiguity here, with the exception of the Wilson item where, as it turned out, it was Mr Wilson who was being rebuked, and not – for a change – doing the rebuking.

Sometimes, of course, 'on' can mean several things and becomes a preposition of what the New Literates would call 'polyguity'. In the heading 'Struggle On Wage Claim', on can mean for, against, over, about, with, after, in, of, towards, or away from. Without reading the news-story it is difficult to know which of these ten other prepositions is covered by one in the heading. Experience of labour relations in this country, however, suggests that the wage-claim struggle story needed the lot.

Since very occasionally on is the correct preposition to use in a heading – as in 'Vicar On Serious Charge', or 'Nation On Tenterhooks' – the only safe substitute would

be the word 're'. It would cover every situation and stimulate curiosity in almost any story except one about wage claims. It would certainly avoid the ambiguity of a heading like 'N. Vietnam Bars Visit by Callaghan', but, to be fair, in doing so it would deprive us of a heading that was intriguing enough to make me read the story below eagerly. I was disappointed; there was nothing in it about Mr Callaghan visiting bars in South East Asia.

Something like 'Re Callaghan Asian Visit' would have put an unenthralling story in its place, and spared thousands of readers unnecessary frustration.

5

It Says Here...

If Fleet Street sub-editors have trouble with their prepositions, they have absolutely none in creating one of
the greatest glories of the English-language Press – the
ambiguous heading.

This is the result of the peculiar eccentricities of English
spelling, and I believe is not found in other countries
where the confusion created by so many verbs and
nouns being spelt in exactly the same way does not exist.

One of the classic examples dates back all of fifty
years now, to a London evening paper's 'Rich Widow Will
Suit'. But the double-take heading still flourishes. In
addition to Mr Callaghan's thwarted pub-crawl, there
are intriguing titles among BBC radio programmes, like
'Bach's Organ Works' (lucky old Bach, I say).

The real puzzles, however, are headings where the
words might be adjectives as well as nouns or verbs.
What can one make of the *Financial Times'* 'Heating For
Old Bill Fails'? Who is old Bill? Why did his heating fail?

The story itself proved an anticlimax. 'Heating for old'
was a three-word description of a Bill in Parliament, and
would have been clearer for having been hyphenated
'Heating-for-old'.

Hyphens which might make things clearer, however, are something of a luxury in modern newspapers. But not even hyphens could make the following heading intelligible at a first reading: 'Civil Servants Pay Benefits'.

Civil is an adjective, servants is a noun. Pay can be a noun, a verb and a form of adjective, benefits can be a noun or a verb. This means that either the Civil Servants' pay will benefit, or that they will pay benefits. It could also mean that there are benefits known as Civil-Servants'-pay benefits, as distinct from, say, overtime-pay benefits.

The news item told us, though not very clearly, what we could never have guessed from the heading:

'Social security benefits [noun] increases [noun] due on October 1 will be paid by [I'll bet that 'by' instead of 'to' surprised everyone] members of the Civil and Public Services Association.'

It cannot be too strongly stressed that the Coarse Linguist is not against changes in the English language. So long as they add to its colour and expressiveness he welcomes them, for what could be more colourful and expressive than the recent addition to the vocabulary of the verb 'to chat-up'? It is a brilliant phrase.

What he does not welcome are changes for the worse – the result of sloppy thinking, and the acceptance of meaningless fashionable phrases merely because they are fashionable, and regarded as some sort of verbal status-symbol. Who but a verbal snob out to impress the illiterate imagines that 'as of now' means anything more than 'at present'?

Between the two extremes there is a form of experimental language which is what one might call primitive English. It is the verbal counterpart of the painting of the

46

Douanier Rousseau, and full of the colour and expresssive-
ness which give a language its character.

The experimental quality of the language is very much
a matter of hit-and-miss. Sometimes the experiments
lead to accidental discoveries as when Ron, who tills and
cossets our garden for us two evenings a week, told us he
would use the spray instead of the watering-can to kill the
pearlwort on the lawn.

The spray, he said, would make it 'more mistified'.
It was a happy invention, making one word do the work
of two.

A BBC local radio announcer, on the other hand,
distinguished himself by saying that he was doing
somebody a disservice instead of an injustice – obviously
the result of not knowing which cliché to use and not
understanding the meaning of either. This was ignorance,
not invention, though.

It was a BBC reporter, however, who first set me thinking of a game with endless possibilities – the no-prefix
game played seriously. P. G. Wodehouse's classic reference
to a character who, if not actually disgruntled, was far
from being gruntled was, after all, a literary conceit.

My BBC reporter was in dead earnest when he related
that the cause of so many 'crisises' in the British motor
industry was 'lack of ertia'.

For those who feel a little homework is needed before
joining the BBC news staff, the following nouns may be of
some help in gumming up the language and adding some
brand new ambiguities as well:

Old Style	*BBC Style*
inbreeding	lack of breeding
increase	lack of crease
indifference	lack of difference

47

Old Style	*BBC Style*
indignation	lack of dignation
indolence	lack of dolence
indulgence	lack of dulgence
inferiority	lack of feriority
iniquity	lack of iquity
intent	lack of tent
infantile	not fantile

One word that will not keep to the rules is inebriety. It is no good standing up in court on a charge of inebriety and insisting that, on the contrary, you were in a state of perfect ebriety. They catch you both ways because, with a disappointing lack of logic, the two words mean the same thing.

For this reason inebriated could not, of course, be used in the Wodehouse Process of Deprefixization of Adjectives.

In any case, this process is best performed with the prefix dis-, as with people

who, if not actually	*are far from being*
distracted	tracted
distraught	traught
disturbed	turbed
disappointed	appointed
disrupted	rupted
distressed	tressed
discreet	creet

It is a game that many will find, if not actually intriguing, at any rate far from triguing.

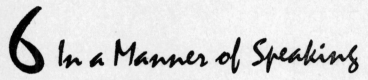

6 In a Manner of Speaking

He multiplieth words without knowledge

JOB 32. 16

There are some aspects of modern English which even the Coarse Linguist is unlikely to be able to master, though to do so might well help him to earn a living in what appear to be the lucrative professions – among them, public relations, the City, and trade union office.

These aspects are nevertheless worth studying by anybody interested in what education and the copycat instinct is doing for the English people before it finally does for the English language.

The two most common forms, both as fascinating in a masochistic way as watching men drill a hole in the road, are Conditionalism and Unconditionalism.

Conditionalism

This is a comparatively recent development in oral English and is based on the belief that one should never be too definite in one's views – or shall we say, never *appear* to be too definite. This, of course, happens only on radio and television. Elsewhere, at strike meetings and other democratic assemblies, manners are not so good or behaviour so tolerant.

D

In ordinary interviews the question 'Do you think . . .?' is answered, not directly with 'I think . . .', but evasively and modishly with 'I would think . . .'

Anybody not used to this new idiom might imagine that the answerer did not actually think but would think, if he could think – that is, if he ever thought at all, which, after hearing his answer, seems very unlikely.

Sometimes 'Do you think . . .?' gets answered by 'I should think . . .' – meaning apparently that the speaker ought to think, but obviously wasn't thinking just then.

At other times 'Do you think . . .?' is answered by 'I would say . . .' – as though the speaker would say if he were asked. But he *is* being asked, so the phrase is just as silly as the others.

Unconditionalism

Unlike Conditionalism, this feature of modern English is the result of a grammatical blind spot – a kind of sub-junctivitis. Ignorance of forms (or refusal to use them) like 'as if it were' or 'as though it were' lead to such gems as the splendid remark about Fred Trueman on p. 35.

For the sake of fairness, however, it must be said that half-literacy is not quite as bad as it sounds, for it often guarantees things being half right – which is not a bad average these days. Our local radio station, which emits a constant stream of verbal surprises, came out with one which was typically half right, because though the use of the subjunctive was correct, the speaker picked the wrong one in the phrase 'Should I wanted it . . .' (This is perhaps not surprising at a station where, on a very hot day, the announcer-chatterer said he thought all houses ought to be installed with showers.)

Hearing in the 1970s the sort of sub-standard English

that was the subject of ghastly class-conscious jokes in *Punch* a hundred years ago, and still found there before the last war, it is obvious that in spite of the money spent on education the English are still just not as at home with their language as the French, Italians, and Germans are with theirs. Considering the English language and its appalling complications, however, perhaps this isn't altogether surprising.

What is more surprising, however, is that, with a language so rich in expressive monosyllables and so capable of vivid imagery created by the simplest and most direct means, so many who speak it will not, as it were, allow it to speak for itself.

And when they try to, they simply get it wrong. Unconditionalism breaks in, and you read in *The Times* a BEA (as it was then) advertisement about Cyprus, with a line about Leonardo da Vinci sending to the island for lace for Milan Cathedral, 'Was he here today, he might well do the same.'

Where else in the world would a State airline need its essay corrected for bad grammar?

Élitism

The French definition of their own word *élite* (from *élire*, to choose or elect) is 'Ce qu'il y a de meilleur, de plus distingué' – or, in our clumsy language, 'what there is of best, of most distinguished'.

The élite of modern English speech and literature, however, are neither chosen nor elected; they appoint themselves, being born to recognize that they are what there is of best, of most distinguished.

They speak French, of course – that is, they use French words. Their English is full of rather grand words taken from rather grand books they've never actually read, mostly by Jung and Freud. They talk about the artist's *persona* with such persistence that one fears the poor man will be charged with indecent exposure, which would predictably, if not arguably, be a traumatizing experience.

Avoidance of the obvious word is what gives élite English its arcane charisma, and enables those who speak it to wallow in the broad spectrum of such luxuries as dichotomy, expertise, catalyst, catharsis (if only those who talk about it would take one), ambience, perceptive, seminal, simplistic, and syndrome. Particularly syndrome which, until you see the word written down, sounds just like a new euphemism for a brothel.

In its way, syndrome is a word of ill-fame, if not actually a disorderly word, though I suppose that, like a brothel, it fulfils a need for those who are not satisfied by the simple pleasures they can get at home of putting phrases into their own words. But then élitism, and the struggle to achieve it, is the most familiar language syndrome of our time.

Status Language

Inhabiting a slightly different intellectual world from the élitists, but no less eager to show off, is that ever-increasing breed of strivers and strainers known as 'executives'.

The executive's position is apparently most coveted by the ambitious youth of today. At least, that is the conclusion I draw from the number of police court cases where the occupation of 'company director' is given by defendants who, not so many years ago, would have described themselves as salesmen, labourers or commission agents.

What companies these proliferating executives direct is

rarely discussed in court. Company director, like esquire (or 'model' for tart), is obviously a courtesy title which the authorities let pass as a harmless fancy.

It is the executive, of course, who does more than most to spread phrases like 'as of now', and pretends that in some way 'not a viable proposition' is more 'meaningful' than 'won't pay', and 'increased profitability' than 'higher profits'. The present price of something is the 'going price'; time is a 'time-scale'; guidance is 'guidelines'; continuing is 'on-going'. They no longer just tell anybody anything, they 'spell it out in depth'; they do not agree, they 'go along with'; they say 'in excess of' for 'more than' and 'utilize' for use; and instead of being jealous and proud of their reputation, prefer to worry narcissistically over their 'image'.*

It was the American executive, of course, who first exploited the suffix '-wise' with such little wisdom to make flashy adverbs of nouns that were minding their own business. The habit was brilliantly parodied soon after it started by Gene Kelly in a film, and immediately adopted seriously by English businessmen anxious to smarten themselves imagewise.

The life and work (or *œuvre*) of the modern executive is a fascinating subject, but unfortunately too big to study here. I would, however, like to remark briefly how much I envy them their hi-fi systems.

Examining the advertisements clearly directed at them by the coloured supplements and glossies (nobody else but hairdressers could afford them) you will note that none of this imposing apparatus works by electricity. There is never a lead or a plug socket in sight, and the

---

* I was shocked to see Marghanita Laski, whom I regard as a trustee of the English language, writing in the *Observer*: 'The most I myself would go along with is to agree that . . .' That is no way for a lexicographer to write. Or is she an executive in her spare time?

record player has no visible wires connecting it with the stereo speakers at all. It just shows what money can buy if you have enough of it to spare for the Japanese – a gas-fired, infinitophonic hi-fi system.

The executive is not only a dealer in his dialect of the English language; he is also a consumer of it, and a considerable industry has developed – sorry, escalated – to supply him with the sort of writing he understands, or is eager to emulate.

The most popular words are 'mystique' and 'viable', neither of which he understands, but uses because they look pretty and sophisticated. The women's page of *The Times* not long ago produced a feature with the blurb: ' . . . Is the domestic freezer even viable in the average eight feet square kitchen of today [no question mark]. In an attempt to uncover some of the mystique associated with domestic freezing in this country, here is a step-by-step guide to choosing, buying and equipping a modern freezer.'

By viable, of course, the writer means practical; but what mystique is supposed to mean only she and her editor know. The danger of vogue words (and executive English is full of them) is that so often they no longer mean what the rest of us thought they meant. And vogue words aren't necessarily always English either.

The Spanish word *patio*, for instance, is used generously by the executive classes to describe what is generally a ground floor terrace, sometimes a verandah, but never a *patio*, because that is an internal courtyard open to the sky. Some owners of what they think is a *patio* have even been heard to give it the exotic alternative name of *hacienda* (with the 'c' lisped as 'th', of course), without realizing that it is the Spanish for an estate, plantation, factory or works.

American phrases, although made up of English words,

55

are so often misused and misunderstood that they might be foreign too. The most notorious example of this was about the time of Munich in 1938, when Sir Samuel Hoare exhorted the country not to be 'jitterbugs', thinking that the American word meant people who were nervous, scared or jittery.

To anybody who knew America the word could hardly have been less appropriate, as it described the youngsters who danced in the entirely extrovert, unscared and joyous manner to the jazz of the Harlem dance halls of the time.

With this precedent in mind it is hardly surprising that American idioms adopted as executive dialect should sometimes misfire. Take this example of advertisers' misplaced fashionableness: 'With hard water . . . your skin is left feeling dry and rough. Your hair is left feeling dry, dull and not as soft as it might be. With soft water you miss out on these little problems . . .' But to 'miss out on' means that you have failed to get, or are unsuccessful in doing, something; it doesn't mean what the advertiser was trying to tell you – that the little problems would be avoided or just not arise. The sentence, in fact, is a good example of missing out on the meaning of missing out.

The American use of the verb to loan, where we say to lend, is also a trap for those advertisers who haven't really studied American usage. I read this the other day: 'Ask your garden shop if you can loan a Fisons spreader.' Used like that the word loan means nothing in any language. It might mean something in America if you wanted to loan a spreader to a friend, but as he isn't mentioned in the advertisement it is unlikely your garden shop would know what on earth you were talking about.

Fisons should tell their advertising agency to try the word 'borrow' sometime. It's old-fashioned, of course, but Americans still use it.

From time to time the executive class makes an important contribution, tantamount to A Breakthrough, to the rationalization of the English language. (Rationalization, as all good executives know, is the means by which the consumer is deprived of what he is used to by a policy of lowering standards to make more money.)

'Cutting out the dead wood' is one of the basic clichés of rationalization. Exactly what constitutes dead wood is a matter of opinion – especially to those who lose their jobs in the cause of rationalization and everybody who gets undrinkable keg beer as a result – but the last place one would expect to encounter the process is in the 'area' of the English language, particularly since rationalizationists thrive on creating dead-wood words, instead of cutting them out.

Nevertheless, they have discovered, and work to death, one word which can be used in place of at least ten other words. It is the verb 'to structure'. This renders obsolete verbs like create, cause, raise, build, make, construct, design, build up, invent, manufacture, and arrange.

There is no doubt that it is an extremely rationalizationary word, and I'll bet the translators of the New English Bible wish they'd thought of it. It would have made their task of taking all the poetry out of the Authorized Version much easier if they could have started off at Genesis 1. 1 with 'In the beginning God structured the heaven and the earth', and gone on to 'Upon this rock I will structure my church'.

Blake could do with a bit of rationalization, too. Up-dated lines that would read

> And was Jerusalem structured here
> Among these dark Satanic mills?

would be a great improvement.

You can structure almost anything, from a situation to a climax, from a price rise to a question in the House of Commons, from a wedding reception to a time-table. You can certainly structure a programme, and you do it by using the sort of jargon the Government minister used after the TU 144 crash at the 1973 Paris Air Show, when he consoled the world with the assurance that anything to be learnt from the inquiry would be 'fed into the Concorde programme'.

The idiom has possibilities. A host would write: 'Please

let me know if you can come to dinner, and I will feed it into my programme.'

One hopes that the guest as well as the programme will be fed.

B.Sc. Talk

While executives and ministers may talk of 'feeding programmes', the term itself does not really belong to the world of business and politics. It is pure B.Sc. talk.

In some ways B.Sc. talk is easy to learn. You just speak as though you were dictating a thesis. You actually *say* 'i.e.' and 'cf.' and 'e.g.' – under the perverse illusion that in some way it is quicker and more scientific to use the initial letters of Latin words you don't understand, or have even heard of, than to say the same thing in English disyllables: 'that is', 'compare', 'frinstance'.

Other favourite conceits are 'viz', which is preferred to 'namely', and 'etcetera' which, to their regret they cannot shorten in speech to 'etc.'. (That 'and so on' is English and a syllable shorter than etcetera is beside their point, of course.)

If the above examples of B.Sc. talk are comparatively easy to learn, there are other 'areas' of the language which are far from being so. Indeed, one begins to suspect that B.Sc.'s are born not made. Certainly to parody their peculiar idiom is almost impossible. The original is pure parody already.

Leaving aside the classic 'high coefficient of slip' for a slippery surface, could you, or anybody you know, describe a bird's singing as (and I quote from a radio programme) 'song-output', and use 'synchronously' to say that the birds were all singing at once?

You couldn't make it up. Any more than you could

make up that other word which has entered the subhuman jargon of hi-fi: 'quadraphonic'. This is top-hole B.Sc. stuff, showing characteristic difficulty in making a new word out of one classical language instead of two. And yet there is a certain lunatic logic in preferring the bastard quadraphonic to the correct Greek-rooted 'tetraphonic' or Latin-rooted 'quadrisonic'.

Few B.Sc.'s seem to know the Greek for four, not having heard of a great race-horse called The Tetrarch, and so not been prompted to ask what the name meant. On the other hand, they know the Latin for four, even if not well enough to remember that it should be quadri- not quadra-. But they are dead scared of using the Latin word sonic, probably because they think people will imagine they are talking about aeroplanes and supersonic flight. So to be safe they call it 'phonic', which they associate with the gramophone and stereophonic recordings.

Of such etymological contortions are new words made.

I am told that at Cambridge all scientists now have to pass a special examination in the use of English before being allowed to enter the university.

And not a moment too soon. The most illustrious of Cambridge graduates can now stop spinning himself dizzy in his grave. Milton! thou shouldst be living at this hour, indeed. Thou knowest not what thou art missing out on.

Effrontism

Bakers and brewers, bouchers and cokes —
For these men doth most harme to the mene puple.
WILLIAM LANGLAND (c. 1330–c. 1400)

Effrontism derives from the French *effronté*, meaning shameless, or brazen-faced, and is used here to describe the practice of uttering such unconvincing euphemisms and excuses that even the most gullible can see them for the barefaced lies they are.

Effrontism (in Italian, *sfrontatismo*) is the speciality of the English shopkeeper, a man of few words and all of them clichés, which he hopes will disguise his indolence and contempt for his customers who, he considers, nevertheless owe him a living.

The most famous example of effrontism is the reply which is now a classic and the subject of cartoons in the comics: 'I'm sick and tired of telling people there's no demand for it.'

Unlike some other effrontist answers this may in fact have been the result of two different causes. If you hear it when asking in vain for real English bitter beer, brewed to be drawn from the wood as God intended, it means that the brewers have been merging and rationalizing again, and have decided that there is more money in giving the English what they don't want than what they do.

If you hear it at a grocer's, a men's outfitters or a draper's, it means that the shopkeeper is too idle to re-order what he has run out of.

He will then try and sell you something you don't want (otherwise you'd have asked for it in the first place), by assuring you in an ingratiating manner that 'We sell a lot of these.' That you do not consider those words much of a recommendation, or the goods offered anything of an adequate substitute, or believe a single word of the sales talk is clear from your whole expression. You are met with a look of pained incredulity by the shopkeeper, and that is the last thing you'll meet in that shop. You never go there again.

One of the most obstinate cases of effrontism is en-countered when, after you have spent a childhood, adolescence and long married life in unswerving devotion to a particular brand of bitter chunky marmalade, the makers are taken over and rationalized, and the flavour and texture of the marmalade becomes such a caricature of its past splendour that it might have been made in France.

Your decision never to buy the brand again is met, not only by the shopkeeper's obligatory look of pained incredulity, but by his Bible-sworn oath that its flavour and quality are just the same as they always were.

Of course, they sell a lot of it; and, of course, there have been no complaints. Particularly there have been no complaints.

This final cliché is the last word in effrontism: it is probably true. The English don't complain. They either know it doesn't do the slightest bit of good in the supermarket-keg-beer-boiled-bread age we live in, or their

palates have been so anaesthetized by keg beer, boiled bread, fish fingers and the constant sucking of sweets, that they literally cannot tell butter from margarine.

Taste, like everything else, is being 'phased out'. There is no demand for it.

Union Officials, Politicians and Other Performing Seals

There is no doubt that to trade union officials and politicians the cliché is the staff of life, as indeed it is to all who have publicly to excuse their behaviour and make an impression on the unsophisticated. Nobody is quicker to catch on to the vogue phrase, to misquote through ignorance, and disfigure the English language.

The use of clichés by public men is nothing new, of course. It is as old as politics itself. What is new is the hitherto unheard-of dissemination of clichés through The Media of Communication.

High among the casters of linguistic pearls cultured in crocodiles' tears, are those who address the nation in times of 'industrial action'.

During a recent strike by one of the nationalized industries (I forget which) a trade union leader assured us of his union's intention to do its utmost 'not to trouble the public inconveniencewise'. The assurance would have been more convincing if the union had held its strike in midsummer, instead of midwinter, but their need for more money was apparently immediate. The reason was what the official described as 'the escalation of inflation'.

By what physical process inflation can be 'escalated' I have no idea. It certainly sounds an easier method of blowing up a tyre than using a pump. Perhaps soon we shall be able to inflate an escalation too. The prospect merits a long cool look, if not actually a long hard cool look. However, that is something needing what Government hand-outs call 'a full and frank discussion', which is guaranteed to prove 'extremely useful'.

If the talks should fail, of course, the situation will be exacerbated and there will be an up-surge of almost everything owing to market forces.

Sometimes it is worth looking up one of the more popular words in the dictionary, just to check that you were right in your interpretation. There was that best-selling word 'pragmatic', for instance. It was used almost as a title for Mr Harold Wilson. As one might refer to the Venerable Adam Bede, it was the Pragmatic Harold Wilson.

The Concise Oxford Dictionary definition of pragmatic and its derivatives was most interesting:

Pragmatic/al, aa. Meddlesome; dogmatic.
Pragmatism, n. Officiousness; pedantry.
Pragmatize, -ise, v.t. Represent as real; rationalize (myth).

There seems to have been some other, philosophical meaning to 'pragmatism', but we were dealing with politics, not philosophy, so – as with the other entries – the first two definitions seemed to be enough for any ordinary person.

Occasionally extra spice is added to the porridge of political language in the form of a good malapropism. Mr Edward Heath came out with one worthy of the form's inventor, the earlier M.P. Richard Brinsley Sheridan, when he referred to 'flaunting' instead of 'flouting' the law. Or was it in fact a malapropism? It's so difficult to tell these days.

Another condiment that gives piquancy to the porridge is the misquotation. This indeed is a matter of obstinate pride to those who consider it pedantic and superciliously intellectual to quote anything correctly.

In spite of compulsory education and two-a-penny degrees at Oxford, they still believe, for the purposes of attacking the Budget or the Opposition for attacking it, that Shakespeare said 'gild the lily' instead of paint it; made assurance doubly, instead of double, sure; and that we were such stuff as dreams are made 'of', instead of 'on'.

Thomas Gray comes in for some particularly obstinate maltreatment. Nothing will persuade the persistent misquoter (who has never looked at the context and thinks it is Shakespeare, anyway) that it was all that glisters that wasn't gold, not glitters. And as for pursuing the even tenor of their way – well, perhaps they have a point there. To speak, as Gray did, of the noiseless tenor is obviously carrying poetic licence too far.

As anybody with two ears to hear with knows, there is unfortunately no such thing as a noiseless tenor.

E

7

Force Majeure

Choice words and measured phrase above the reach
Of ordinary men; a stately speech . . .

WORDSWORTH

One of the results of joining 'Europe' (as it is now called to distinguish it from what used to be known to us, and still is to the Corsicans, as the Continent), has been a remarkable up-surge in the spirit of the Entente Cordiale.

At least, I suppose that's what it is, since there is no doubt that, like that ugly-looking aeroplane with the unfortunately cynical name, Anglo-French co-operation is pretty active these days.

The English police, for instance, have obviously been invited by the French to use their VHF stations whenever they wish.

To those of us in the south of England this is a most convenient arrangement. It enables us, while we are enjoying the broadcasts from the Normandy coast of France-Musique, France-Culture, or France-Inter, to keep up to date, from minute to minute, with the activities of the police of such far-flung places as High Wycombe, Ealing and Canterbury, and so be constantly reassured that the public safety is ever in the thoughts of its guardians. (For Coarse Linguists one of the major pleasures of listening to the French radio is to hear announcers who, if they aren't so hot at pronouncing other

66

people's, can at least pronounce their own language. Which is more than they can do at the BBC – except in the World Service, where they broadcast to foreigners.)

We are also reassured by the French network that Policeman's English is still very much what it was and unaffected by the knavish tricks practised on our unhappy mother tongue by professional writers and broadcasters.

Those of us who have ever heard evidence given by a policeman in a police court, or been charged there with knocking off policemen's helmets on Boat Race Night, are familiar with the carefully measured manner in which policemen tell their tales.

What few of us could have guessed is that policemen use the same sort of language when talking to each other on walkie-talkies or on their car radios. It is their instinctive form of communication when there's constabulary duty to be done, though, of course, they may well talk to their wives the same way when they're at home.

The basic principle of police language is to use long words and as many of them as possible, to say the simplest things. The Dignity of the Law must not only be upheld; it must be heard to be upheld.

After long and careful study of what I hear on France-Musique, it is clear that certain questions are always asked and certain statements always made with what can only be the officially recommended sequences of words, as immutable as the questions in a marriage ceremony.

If the questioner wants to know where P.C. Comble is, he asks him over the blower: 'Will you please inform me of your location?'

P.C. Comble, having informed the inquirer of his location, is then asked whether he is able to locate a vehicle called a 'Capree' (Index number Foxtrot Charlie Delta 186 Delta). He will do his best, he says, but he is 'not cognizant of the area'. He will, however, shortly 'ascertain the details and proceed to the location'.

Later, P.C. Comble will be asked if he needs any 'assistance in acquiring further information appertaining to the incident'. The constable will reply no thanks: the 'incident is terminated'.

As P.C. Comble continues to drive his mobile unit around the area, the voice on the blower tells him that a caller has 'requested the attendance of the police', and would P.C. Comble 'please inquire as to whether anybody has any knowledge as to the location of the address'.

P.C. Comble replies: 'Will do' – which is about as near

as the mobile police force ever gets to saying yes.

Policeman's talk is a fascinating example of a firmly established traditional manner of speech. It is not strictly a jargon, for every word spoken is common English usage and certainly none of them is peculiar to police talk – except for malapropisms due to over-eager elaboration of unnecessary words.

A recent broadcast on France-Culture was enlivened by an interval talk given by a mobile unit who reported that a colleague was in the car park 'taking informationary numbers' – a smart example of high-sounding nonsense. Why should anybody take numbers except for 'informationary' purposes – if there were such a word, which there isn't?

Research into the origins of police talk has so far been unproductive. It doesn't seem to be inspired by chief constables – at least, not in my experience. The only two chief constables I have ever known well were quite appalled by the flat-footedness of their constables' English.

It was as though, one of them said, somebody had gone to Roget's *Thesaurus* and looked up all the longest synonyms for the commonest words, and had formed a special vocabulary for the Force out of them.

Starting with 'proceed' for 'go' or 'walk', the highlights of the vocabulary include:

The Police say	We say
request	ask
assistance	help
require	want *or* need
cognizant	know
ascertain as to whether	find out *or* see if
locate	find
in the vicinity of	near
adjacent to	next to

69

The Police say	We say
very adjacent to	near
location	place
terminated	settled *or* finished
inform	tell
acquiring further information	finding out more
appertaining to	about
requested the attendance of the police	sent for the police
as to why	why
as to where	where
as to how	how

The repertoire is endless. Which makes one think it must be nice to be a policeman and have all that time to use so many long and unnecessary words. Only those who know how to make the most of their leisure could afford to say, 'We have a lack of information on this at the moment.'

When they are not speaking on France-Musique or France-Culture, the English police speak to us on local BBC wavelengths. Radio London has regular contributions from local police officials who, of course, show their metropolitan breeding. A police spokesman said about traffic jams in Earls Court that they had had a letter about it from the Home Office: 'It was quite a normal sophisticated approach', he told us.

Who first compiled the standard police vocabulary, however, is still not known for certain. One theory is that it is the work of generations of sergeants, and as every constable wants to be a sergeant he apes the sergeant's manner of speaking and keeps the vocabulary in general use.

Unfortunately, we have a lack of information on this at the moment.

8   *Europa v Bull (J.)*

. . . Snakes with double tongue

SHAKESPEARE

It was in fact the police who first made me wonder if in 'joining Europe', we really knew what we were letting ourselves in for.

Not long after Entry, I read of a wanted bank-robber who 'spoke with a European accent'. I found this most disquieting.

If speaking with a European accent was an important clue to the identity of the robber, it meant that the rest of us could now be suspected of robbing banks because we, too, all spoke with European accents. For however much the TUC may dislike it, it is an unfortunate and inescapable fact that ethnically, culturally and geographically we are Europeans, and have actually been so for millions of years – and not just since 1 January 1973.

We are used to being thought by Americans to speak our own English language with an English accent, and by most other foreigners to speak *their* languages with an English accent. But it is something quite new and bewildering to find that, like our fellow-Europeans, we now speak everybody else's language with the same accent as they do, since we are Europeans and must therefore have European accents. Q.E.D.

As good Coarse Linguists, of course, we are the last people to encourage Lingoism, or the refusal to speak, or try to speak, any language except one's own. There are times, however, when it is a matter of simple courtesy to speak English to foreigners, and that is when they visit us with the firm intention of learning our language – God help them.

And it needs God to help them to distinguish the subtleties of stressing the right syllables of the English language, let alone sort out its dark Satanic spelling and its pronunciation, for not even those custodians of our oral heritage, the BBC itself, can tell when to say *in*crease or in*crease*, *con*flict or con*flict*, *trans*fer or trans*fer*, *in*cline or in*cline*.

But it is that inbred, perfidious ambiguity of the English which comes out in their language and floors that wretched invisible export, the foreigner.

How can they ever learn to recognize the subtle difference between a word used with an optimistic implication, and the same word with a pessimistic one?

To say that there is 'a remote possibility', for instance, is more optimistic than to say that 'the possibility is remote'.

Again, even the most experienced English reader of advertisements in *The Times* can never be sure when he reads that 'A few seats are available' for some function or other, whether that is better than, or the same thing as, a similar announcement without the indefinite article.

Does 'Few seats available' mean, as I believe, that there are even fewer seats than 'a few' suggests? Or is the advertisement stripped of the indefinite article merely to save the cost of an insertion charged for by the word?

Then the unfortunate foreigner, having failed entirely

to sort out the difference between few and a few, is faced with the completely puzzling phrase 'quite a few'.

Except that logic doesn't enter into the English language in any form, it would be logical to imagine that quite a few was a fairly moderate amount of fewness – just as quite warm implies moderate warmth, or, in England, an eccentric improvement of normal summer weather.

But quite a few means quite a lot, and so does quite a bit. Could anything be more Englishly (we need an adverb like that) non-committal, vague and understated?

Often, of course, such phrases are clearly designed to puzzle the foreigner who, after all, must not be encouraged to speak our language too well, or he could become a serious security risk.

He will spend a lifetime trying to master the difference between 'slowing up' and 'slowing down', and nothing will ever convince him that there *is* no difference – not even his understandable belief that, as Noël Coward sang, the English are 'obviously definitely Nuts!' Nor is life made any easier for him to know that it is possible to slow up going downhill and to slow down going uphill. Or that when he is asked in a pub to drink up his half-empty glass and have another he is just as likely to be asked to drink down his half-full glass and have the same again.

These are English idioms sent merely to plague the foreigner and try his patience. There are others, however, which might have been specially designed to insult him – or so he might think.

There is a true case, which happened not long after the War, when John Christie, the founder of Glyndebourne, repaid hospitality he had received in Vienna, by taking his Viennese host to lunch at his St James's Street club.

Even by the standards of post-war austerity (which

were quite something) it was a pretty unappetizing lunch, the high spots of the menu being a vegetable pie and rice pudding.

On parting after the meal, the Viennese thanked his host for his kindness.

'My dear Freddi,' was the reply, 'it was the least I could do!'

Freddi didn't know what to say. The meal had certainly been awful and it was more than likely that his English host could not have offered anything less attractive, but why was it necessary for him to say so?

It was a long time before Freddi discovered what Christie had meant, and even now he is not wholly convinced by the explanation.

The ambiguities of spoken English can be an endless puzzle, not only to foreigners, but also to the Scots, Irish, Welsh and Americans, particularly when faced with the Englishman's lazy habit of not aspirating his 'w's' when he should.

I once got involved in a cross-purposes discussion with a young lady who told me she was reading a fascinating book about Wales. I told her I'd been to Cardiff and Mountain Ash once, but I didn't know the country well.

'Oh, this isn't about Wales,' she said. 'It's about Wales – those fish things.'

Certainly, English is no worse than French in its number of phonetically identical words often only distinguishable by their context or their spelling – like *cent* and *sans*, or *dent* and *dans*, or *ver* (worm), *vers* (towards), *vert* (green), *vair* (miniver), *verre* (glass) and *vers* (verse).

On the other hand, the English reduce to the same phonetic sound words which are not intended to sound the same, and are not so pronounced by Celts and Americans. The average Englishman tends to feel hurt if, when he talks to you about 'waw', you ask which 'waw' he means – Evelyn or Second World? And sometimes not even context can help you to understand what he means when he talks about 'lore and order', or a 'saw place'.

Many ambiguities are merely in the eye of the beholder, of course, and though anybody knowing modern French would, on quick reflection, understand what was meant by them, we were once pardonably surprised to be confronted by two signs a hundred yards apart on the same French road reading 'Bar Camping!' and 'Stop Camping!'

What kind of puritanism was this, we wondered, that produced such intolerant slogans? Perhaps it was the work of the untiring Mme Blanchemaison, guardian of the · moral welfare of the French.

Whoever was responsible for the threatening signs on Route Nationale 7, a few miles further along was a sign showing that French hospitality was still what it used to be. Outside a restaurant in Cannes was the announcement 'On demand personnel féminin'. The thought that perhaps the final 'e' had dropped off the second word was quickly dismissed as being unlikely. There would be no point in advertising for female personnel, except for the obvious purposes, in a restaurant which was an obstinately self-service establishment. It was a welcome whiff of the oo-la-la's to encourage the English after the other two depressing signs.

Sometimes foreign signs convey their message to the English traveller with unusual speed, although they may not be addressed to him. On Spanish roads you encounter the firm instructions, '¡ No use klaxon!' (The exclamation mark upside down at the beginning is so that if you're standing on your head you won't miss it.)

We felt rather insulted when we first saw this. It was insulting, I mean, to be addressed in broken English as

though we wouldn't understand ordinary English. (Recalling the Barcelona menus written in what the Spanish imagine is English, they were probably right – we wouldn't.) On reflection, however, we came to the conclusion that the word 'use' was not a verb but a noun, and that 'klaxon' was a verb not a noun, and that we were being informed that it was no use klaxoning.

This hopeless observation seemed reasonable as nearly every human and mechanical object found on Spanish roads is as deaf as a post and twice as obstinate.

After some further thought, it struck us that the sign was in Spanish, and that in their usual *caballero* manner the natives were unconcerned that tourists might not understand. Nor might they, if they were French or

76

German; but as it happened, with the notice consisting of three English words, the English *did* get the hang of it, so sucks to them . . .

Out of the struggles of the foreigner with the English language there often emerges a refreshing honesty which is not what the writer intended. For instance, I know of no clearer warning of what to expect in the restaurant of the French Newhaven–Dieppe car ferry than the claim that it serves meals 'at most elaborated rates'. (Even if what they meant by *élaborer* was 'carefully work out', not 'elaborate', it was still a little bluntly put.)

And then there is the chain of quick service restaurants in Paris which is proud to serve you 'baked fish-shell' – as honest a way as I know of describing what is too often served up as *Coquille St Jacques*, otherwise fish in ashtrays.

If it is any consolation to foreigners, there are examples in English of ambiguity so complex that even the natives don't understand them. As we have come to expect, these ambiguities – multiguities, even – flourish most prolifically in the newspapers, where headings are usually designed to give the reader an inkling of the subject and nature of the stories below them.

However, the guess of the most experienced foreign speaker of English is as good as ours when it comes to deciphering the recent heading which ran:

PRESCRIBING
FLAWS CHAOS

At a first glance it seemed to mean that the act of prescribing flaws leads to chaos – not unlikely in the circumstances. A second glance suggested that prescribing causes flaws in chaos that would otherwise be a flawless chaos. A third glance – but by then the attention had wandered from the subject of doctors' prescriptions to the unusual heading of another story which discussed 'Well-matched lead dancers in Swan Lake'. Even the context didn't guarantee that 'lead' rhymed with 'read' and not 'read'.

Again, the foreigner's guess is as good as ours when it comes to words whose etym. the dictionary would say was dub. or uncert., if not actually unkn.

One such word appeared in a newspaper description of a house with an extension that consisted of three extra rooms 'plus a vanitory room'.

A really informationary bit of mystique, that one . . .

Ordinary straightforward confusion caused to foreigner and native by the misuse of words is so frequent that it hardly deserves mention. The double-take caused by newspaper double-talk is a fact of life at the breakfast table, but it is difficult to believe that half the things said in the newspapers are really meant. Around the time of the Cup Final an official stated: 'There will be a clean-up on illicit ticket sales as far as possible.' Although he didn't mean it, in fact he spoke nothing but the truth: people do clean up on illicit ticket sales. That's what they're for.

The teasing and baiting of foreigners with the English language does not go unanswered. The French and Germans in particular retaliate by making their spoken numerals unwieldly for Italians and Belgians, as well as for us.

The Germans count like the English up to twenty – one to nineteen having literal equivalents; but thereafter the cardinal and ordinal numbers get too poetic by half – one-and-twenty, four-and-twenty, seven-and-seventieth and so on – making us count as though we were still reciting nursery rhymes, instead of trying to get a good rate of exchange for our sterling.

On the other hand, the Germans who are so wasteful

with their counting make up for it when they come to writing down numbers in so many words. Not in so many words, in fact, but in one word, as though they were trying to keep down the cost of a telegram.

Many years ago, during the historic pre-war German inflation, I had to have my passport stamped with an exit permit. The service cost me 2 700 828 000 marks (which just about bought a cup of coffee at the time), and its receipt was acknowledge in one word: *zweimilliardensiebenhundertmillionenachthundertachtundzwanzigtausendmark.*

The French, for their part, count up orally quite sensibly until they get to the number sixty-nine. Where the other Latin countries then continue logically with words suggesting that seventy is seven tens, the French write 70 but pronounce it sixty-ten, progressing through a

series of numbers that sound like a nightmare tennis score – sixty-fifteen, sixty-sixteen, sixty-nineteen – in which game point is never reached.

Having decided that the number sixty should serve as the prefix for numbers from sixty-one to seventy-nine, the number eighty changes the subject altogether and is called four-twenty, which remains as the prefix from eighty to ninety-nine – from four-twenty-one to four-twenty-nine.

What purpose this French eccentricity serves I have no idea. If people complain that the English are obstinately individual and non-conformist, at least we can count straight and don't involve people in unnecessary mental arithmetic.

In the French spoken by the Belgians the sixties are followed by *septante,* the seventies by *ottante* and the eighties by *nonante*. Except for the last three teen numbers, which are spoken as ten-seven, ten-eight, ten-nine, the Belgians, like the Italians and the Spanish, describe their cardinal numbers in a civilized – that is, English – way.

9 *One Speaks English*

Bless thee! thou art translated

SHAKESPEARE

Membership of the European Economic Community has brought with it one unforeseen hazard: our fellow members' increasing enthusiasm for including English among the languages appearing on goods likely to be imported by this country.

International marketing, particularly of tourism, has long been notorious for its howlers and is the frequent subject of comment in the English gossip and letter columns. That similar howlers made by the English in foreign languages are not so well publicized is largely because the greatest howler committed by the English is their refusal to try to translate anything at all for the benefit of their foreign customers either here or abroad.

Nearly every returning traveller brings back a new item for his collection. Sometimes these items are bizarre, at other times very puzzling indeed (when not utterly incomprehensible), because there is no clue to how their composers arrived at their conclusions, except by a random choice of the wrong word of the many they don't understand in the dictionary.

The Spaniards are on the whole the most prolific authors of howlers and nonsenses. This is because of all their

F

visitors the English have the worst reputation as linguists. But the Spaniards run them pretty close sometimes, as with the couple of dishes I found on a menu in Tarragona, for instance.

One item was listed as 'Lom Chop'. Obviously, you say, a shot at lamb chop. So it might have been if there had been any such thing on the menu, but there wasn't. Lom Chop was offered as a translation of *Tournedos con champignons*, which isn't lamb or a chop in any language.

This dish was part of the *Servicio a la Gran Carta* which also included fish items such as Sea Wolf, Clay-Fish *(langoustines à la chinoise?)* and Several-Fish. On the page not surprisingly headed *Carta Popular* was the intriguingly enigmatic Rape in Fishers Sauce.

The Spanish original was, if anything, no more comforting, for the rape was described, threatened, or promised, as *a la Marinera* – in the sailor's manner. We failed to identify the fish, of course, but it was probably a kind of sea-bream. Mediterranean fish nearly always is.

(In passing, mistyping is responsible for some of the more startling words found on menus and even in one's own home. The first typewriter I ever had was very ancient, but also very lively. It was a machine with a disconcerting habit of jumping a space when certain letters were used – the 'w', the 'e' and the 'o', particularly – so that it w ro te w o rds w ith ho le s in the m. The word Psychotherapist used to come out as 'Psycho the rapist', like a Hitchcock film.)

It was not misprinting or mistyping, however, which enlivened a packet of grated Parmesan made in Italy, bought in France, and with announcements in English, German, French, Dutch and Spanish. The English was worthy of Lewis Carroll, for alone among the languages it was decorated with what might be described as an equation – but one not even Einstein could have solved. It read:

$$\frac{32\%}{\text{on dry matter}} = \frac{3/4 \text{ FEET}}{\text{FAT}}$$

Even if the inclusion of the word 'feet' is explained by supposing that it was the only non-metric unit known to the Italian who composed the problem, one is still no nearer discovering why Feet over Fat should equal 32%.

To make things even more difficult, the only figure mentioned in any of the other languages was 30% in a text that was Dutch and therefore no help as a crib.

The Spanish on the packet, on the other hand, made no mention of any percentage of anything, for it consisted entirely of a eulogy on the unique properties of Parmesan cheese, which was pure Italian propaganda.

The English equation is something quite new in international marketing, of course, and even if to most people it is quite meaningless at least it makes a change, and is certainly no more meaningless than the primitive English normally found in such cases.

There is a curious parsimoniousness common to the businessmen of all nations. They would rather make fools of themselves in a foreign language than pay somebody else a small fee to get it right. This is particularly the case in big tourist centres abroad which are filled with English and American visitors, and where there is often a British consulate or Chamber of Commerce whose members would be only too pleased to help with the local opera house programme synopses, or the restaurants' menus. It is the old story of the ha'porth of tar, however, and considering the ha'porth of tar needn't be more than an occasional free seat or a discount off the price of a meal, the obstinate determination of the enterprises to do it themselves is extremely short-sighted.

Not only short-sighted but very difficult – when the dictionary offers so many different meanings of the same word, which are just as great a trap for the Englishman trying to translate into a foreign language, as for the foreigner trying to translate into English.

Even contexts can't necessarily be guaranteed to make it clear. A Frenchman looking for the English word for *roué* can choose from rake, trickster or consummate diplomat; for *rossignol* from nightingale, pick-lock, unsaleable book or old shopkeeper. An Englishman, looking for the word for rake, might light on the garden tool and translate *The Rake's Progress* as *Le progrès du râteau*, or on meeting *gendarme* for the first time be bewildered by the choice between virago, termagant, flaw, spot, sediment, fur, smoothing iron, red herring and ha'penny cigar.

What must be a record for variety of meaning was an Italian word I once encountered in translating a line from Mozart's *Marriage of Figaro*. In the last act a character comes on with a basket which she tells us contains an apple, a pear, and something called a *ciambella*.

I went to the dictionary to sort out *ciambella* and was faced with a word that could mean

a baby's teething ring
a rubber ring for swimming
a life belt
an air cushion
a kiss-curl
a circular movement of a horse
a knotted ring of cloth worn on the head when carrying a load
the balance wheel in a watch
an ancient kind of military incendiary weapon made of rags
    covered with pitch, wax and oil
a ring-shaped cake
a lavatory seat

I settled for the cake. Babies, swimming, horses, cushions, kiss-curls and lavatory seats didn't altogether suit the context somehow.

At the end of this bit of research, however, I began to feel more sympathetic towards amateur translators and surprised that they do as well as they do in the circumstances. Though I do wish they'd sometimes tell us how they arrive at some of their findings, and what they think they're saying.

There is still in Dieppe a 'tée and caks' establishment that recommends the English visitor (by a permanent painted sign) to try its 'omelette hash green'.

What French word did they ever look up to make 'hash green'? One can imagine an Italian going to a not very comprehensive dictionary to translate *scuola promiscua* and

85

coming out with 'promiscuous school' instead of 'co-educational school', but there is no phrase I know of in French that could produce 'hash green'. Or in English either, come to that.

Unfortunately, I've never met anybody who has eaten that Dieppe omelette to ask them what it was, and I'm certainly not trying it myself. It will just have to remain the Dark Lady of the Sonnets among omelettes.

10 With a Little Help for Our Friends

Although it can take the native Coarse Linguist all his time to know what they mean himself, there are some words and phrases in constant general use in modern English which it is only polite to try to help the foreigner to understand.

Knowing perfectly well that no amount of British commitment to the European Ideal will ever make the Englishman any keener to learn a foreign language, the foreigner has not relaxed his own determination to learn English as an accomplishment required of every normally educated individual.

But however well the foreigner may think he knows the English, he can never be quite sure when a word or phrase is a characteristic understatement or when it is a deliberate exaggeration.

The exaggeration is particularly difficult to spot, because experience has taught the foreigner that understatement is as typical of the Englishman as his classic *sang froid habituel* – once translated as his 'habitual bloody cold'.

Most of the words I have in mind are, of course, more

often found in The Media than in normal balanced conversation.

Drought: Any period of four consecutive days without rain, when public notices appear in local papers threatening life imprisonment if you water your tomatoes.

Heatwave: Any period of four consecutive days without rain, with what could be normal summer weather in every other country in Europe. Workers go on strike because it is too hot.

Chaos: This is caused by snow falling unexpectedly in January, leading to subnormal winter weather which is nothing like as cold as they get in every other country in Europe. Workers go on strike because it is too cold. Non-strikers can't get to work because it is too cold for the trains.

Wintry Showers: These are a mysteriously exaggerated feature of the English weather forecasts from November to March. Except that they fall during these months, it is never explained what – apart from the temperature of you, the air and the rain water – is particularly wintry about them.

Breakthrough: Exaggerated, over-publicized claim for what may or may not prove to be slight technical progress in some field of research, ranging from astronomy and the issue of dog licences by computer, to Post Office sorting. This is usually followed by

Teething Troubles: An understatement used to excuse the failure of almost any much-boasted-about new technical or economic undertaking by a nationalized industry such as railways, gas, electricity. It is also applied to explain the expensive crashes of new aeroplanes, the collapse of motorway bridges and the unwarranted increase in Post Office postage and telephone rates.

Industrial Action: Industrial inactivity.

Industrial Inactivity: Full employment.

Crisis: The original wolf-word cried not once, but many thousands of times too often. It is a word no modern newspaper can do without. At night the Building Societies carefully tell us there is no mortgage rate crisis, the following morning in *The Times* the heading of a front-page story tells us of a Building Society Crisis. All foreigners should ignore the word. We do.

Disgusting: The battle cry of British Democracy, particularly favoured by the working class – that is, lower income bracket – housewife, who uses it whenever interviewed by The Media on the subject of sex, bidets, black people, garlic, or her £50-a-week husband's having to pay income tax.

Seriously Ill: This is not so much an exaggeration as a puzzling euphemism used to describe the condition of a patient seriously hurt in an accident. The term normally used is 'in a serious condition', or 'having serious injuries'. Seriously ill is something the BBC seems to have thought up. Nobody knows why.

Phased out: To say that a product is 'being phased out' means that you can't get it. You decide you'd like to buy another British car like the one you've got. You can't. The model has been phased out, so you buy a foreign one instead.

Run down (vb) : To denigrate.

Run down (vb) : To reduce in number.

Run-down (n) : A reduction in number.

Run down (vb) : To summarize.

Run-down (n) : A summary.

Run down (vb) : To recite a complete list of items.

Run-down (n) : A recital of a complete list of items.

Run down (vb) : To run over a pedestrian.

Run down (vb): To pay a brief visit to the country from London, as in to run down to Brighton for the weekend.

Run down (adj): A clock that hasn't been wound up.

Run down (adj): In need of a holiday.

Stage Irish: This is the brand of English which the English think is spoken by the Irish. It is used facetiously and incorrectly by the Englishman to make (he thinks) the Irishman feel at home. In an accent that he imagines to be Irish, he cries 'Begorrah!' and 'Top of the mahnin' to yez!', and asks 'Would you be after having a drink, at-all, at-all?'

To humour his host – and because he is thirsty – the Irishman will answer yes, and make no comment. Life is too short to explain that the phrase is nonsense. An Irishman will say 'I was after having a drink when . . .' only when, in narrative, he means that he had had a drink and then did, said or thought something or other; or had another jar.

If the foreigner (and I include the English in this) wants to buy an Irishman a drink all he has to say is 'What'll you have?' The phrase will be understood by the Irish drinking classes the world over.

Dog talk: The foreigner will not take long to note that the English not only talk *to* their dogs, but *for* them. It is an idiom without parallel in any other language, so far as I know.

Instead of using the normal third person singular to describe a dog's health the dog-owner will speak of 'our' health, for all the world as if the beast were Queen Victoria doing a Christmas broadcast.

These – I was going to say 'conversations', but 'proclamations' is nearer to it – these proclamations can be most frequently heard in the saloon bars of pubs in the genteeler districts of London, such as South Kensington and Earls

Court, and in other ritualistic gin-and-tonic circles up and down the country on Sunday mornings.

Not even the most casual anonymous visitor dropping into the bar on these occasions can hope to escape attention from the dog-owners, who not only talk endlessly to each other about their animals, but will try to involve the total stranger as well.

'We were *rather* sick last night, Sooty-sooty, weren't we? But we had a powder-wowder and now we're right as rain – aren't we, darling?'

The stranger can only smile wanly and pray he won't sick up; or, if he has the courage, can reply by patting the revolting animal's head and saying: 'We're *rather* beastly, aren't we, darling?' The owner will not notice

what you really said. The stranger used the magic royal and canine We, and is therefore a doggy person too.

The English will also talk to their babies in the same words: 'We were *rather* sick last night, Jennifer-pennyfer, weren't we? But Mummy gave us a *lovely* antibiotic and now we're right as rain – aren't we, darling?'

Fortunately, babies are not yet allowed into the saloon bars of pubs even on Sunday mornings. So at least we can escape *that*.

Owing to public demand: This claim is such a whopping exaggeration that it rates as too barefaced to be included under *Effrontism*.

It is the claim you will hear as an excuse when, instead of getting the beer or mineral water you want in the size you want and have had all your life, you are forced to buy it in 'disposable' bottles containing much less and costing much more than the old ones.

Before the introduction of the 'disposable' bottle, you paid a deposit which was refundable and the bottle was thus made what is called 're-cyclable'. Now you are expected to deal with the potential pollution yourself by having to throw the empties into the dustbin, and are thus encouraged to waste material unnecessarily in a world which is growing critically short of raw materials.

The public, it goes without saying, have naturally never made any such demand. It has not even been consulted, or warned that the old bottles were being 'phased out'. (Phasing-out is always done without warning, for it is a euphemism used to disguise the accomplished fact that production of what you want has already ceased for good and all. The process is designed to restrict the public's choice.)

The claim that 'owing to public demand' you can no longer buy a large tonic or a proper bottle of beer, is not invented by the shopkeeper (though it is invariably repeated by him), but by the big monopolies (or 'con-bines', one might call them) as part of their now familiar policy of treating the public with increasing contempt, increasing prices, and then having the impertinence to say we demanded it.

Personally, I am greatly in favour of one vast merger of all the big breweries. This will make their eventual nationalization by a Labour government much easier, and good riddance. No state-brewed beer could ever be nastier than what is sold now and at least we would not be lining the pockets and bringing smiles to the unaccept-able mugs of hypocrite businessmen.

Furthermore: owing to definitely *unprecedented* public demand, broken biscuits are now universally available ready-packed in cellophane. This is a Great Breakthrough. They used only to be sold loose at half price at the corner grocer's.

Presently: Foreigners must be warned that this is probably the most dishonest word in the English language. Its purpose is entirely to deceive and it expresses neither faith, hope nor charity. It is evasive, deliberately creates false confidence, and lacks preciseness. It is not used as a statement of fact, but as a vague non-committal declara-tion of intent to avoid or delay the fulfilment of what should be a promise.

It is the supreme example of the Englishman's word being accepted by the rest of the world as his bond, and proving to be nothing of the sort.

The English first encounter the word in childhood and, more than anything else, it undermines a child's belief in its parents' honesty.

'Please may I go out and play, Mummy?'

'Not now, darling. Presently.'

'When is presently, Mummy?'

'Eat your pudding, darling, there's a good boy.'

But presently never comes. The word, you begin to learn, is a pure swindle; it has nothing to do with the present. Its whole purpose is a negation of what God intended – that is, an adverb of the present, the here-and-now. As it is, it might in fact mean yesterday Why not? Since, if tomorrow is presently – that is, not the present – yesterday is not the present either.

The Scots, to their eternal and educated credit, still use the word like a civilized and honest people, as the English did happily until the seventeenth century, when for some reason they 're-thought' it, or rationalized it or something. Perhaps to revive the word in this country we should persuade our executives and politicians and mediacraties that it is the very latest American neologism. After all, they swallowed 'hopefully'– so why not presently, which they obviously don't know the meaning of either?

The foreigner, expecting presently to mean what it says, is naturally defeated by the way the English interpret it. If ever there was a word which got the English their reputation for being unable to deliver a suspension bridge or a first-class letter on time, it is presently.

Foreigners have adverbs formed from their words for present, like *présentement, gegenwärtig, presentamente*, which mean what they say. Not unreasonably they expect ours to do the same.

The French even use *actuellement* as a synonym, probably in the hope of nudging us into using 'actually', if we're so stupid about presently. But it does no good. We can't even use actually properly most of the time. It is a fill-up word, signifying nothing, like 'you know' or 'like' or 'see' or 'sort of thing'.

Actually, actually is correctly the adverb formed from

an adjective meaning present or current, and is just what we need. But though nobody has suggested that the word in this sense is actually archaic, the Conc. Ox. Dict. doesn't half tautologize you once you start wondering about saying 'in actual fact'. It seems that 'actual' means 'existing in fact', and 'actually' means 'in actual fact'. So if you say in actual fact what you're saying (in actual fact) is in existing-in-fact fact.

On the whole presently is neater, and I'm glad to see that the Americans (who were speaking good English in the seventeenth century and haven't forgotten it) are beginning to revive it to atone for 'as of now' and 'at this moment in time'. Certainly Churchill wasn't haughty about it, which ought to commend it.

All it needs now is for foreigners to sue any English firm that promises to send the goods presently and doesn't send them at once That is, presently.

Riddles: The foreigner can usually find an idiomatic equivalent in his own language for English proverbs. 'A stitch in time saves nine', for instance, comes out in France as *un point fait à temps épargne cent* – a neater rhyme than ours, and a higher rate of productivity.

The Italians also save a hundred stitches to our nine, but their rhyming is no better than ours: *un punto dato in tempo ne salva cento*. The Germans, a little perversely, mention neither time, stitches nor their number. They change the subject altogether and tell you not to put off till tomorrow what you can do today.

On the other hand, the English riddle is something which we should never wish on any foreigner and it is our duty as hosts to see that he is never involved in one. Translation, however careful, does no good. Explanation is possible, but not really worthwhile, for it can lead to frustrating conversation.

'When is a door not a door?' you ask your French friend, explaining that you are asking a riddle – *'une énigme,'* you add helpfully.

Your explanation is superfluous, for it is met with the familiar hunted look of total incomprehension seen on so many foreign faces in England.

'The answer,' you say, 'is when it's ajar.'

'When the door is a pot?'

'No, when it's ajar.'

'Why if it's a jar? You might as well say "when it's a cricket field or a double bass." A door is a door Isadora Duncan . . .'

'No,' you say patiently and go to the dictionary to look it up. Then:

'Here it is – *entre-bâillée. Quand est-ce-qu'une porte n'est pas une porte? – Quand elle est entre-bâillée.'*

'But how *not* a door? Only a door can be *entre-bâillée* – or a window.'

'Yes, I know. It's a riddle – a joke – for children, you see.'

'I see. Not very funny, even for children.'

'Oh, have a drink . . .'

G

11 *Porsenography*

Lars Porsena of Clusium
By the nine gods he swore

MACAULAY

The trouble with swearing is that it has got such a bad name.

The choice epithet, the rounded oath, the rich four-letter obscenity, and all other forms of imaginative invective, have lost their effectiveness through what can only be described, in the élitist language of the day, as the miasma of over-exposure.

When rude words are no longer taboo in films, on the stage, in print, television and the radio, or even in what was once called Polite Society, they lose all power to shock, and no rude word is any use if it doesn't shock. It merely becomes monotonous.

The famous 'bloody' in Shaw's *Pygmalion* is still a wonderful theatrical moment, even though the word itself has long lost its general power to shock, or even surprise. But because Shaw times it so superbly in its dramatic context, even though the audience waits expectantly for it, it never fails in its great comic effect.

But in real life what is there left to say for the man who has said everything? The Permissive Society has achieved in less than a decade what centuries of censorship and social pressure failed to do. And it is nothing to be grateful for, either: it has left us a language without swear-words.

Perhaps in a generation or so a new set of taboos will evolve, and with it the creation of a new vocabulary of words to swear with. Where blasphemy, sex and the common bodily functions were what modern swearing was based on, a new repertoire may be built up eventually of words derived from whatever religion, or physiological, pathological or anatomical features of the human body are by then considered taboo subjects.

Terms of obscene abuse could include such new rude words as computer, conservationist, priest, footballer, student, tourist, democrat, trade unionist or private patient. To accuse a man to his face of being any of these things could well lead to a breach of the peace and a charge of criminal libel.

This does not mean, however, that the obligatory four-letter word need disappear altogether from the vocabulary of the powerful swearer of oaths and shouter of abusive expletives. The human body, which has supplied us with what society has regarded as obscenities since Adam first called Eve a berk, has plenty in reserve. It would be easy to form a new set of rude words like acne, wart, cyst, gall, boil, ague, noma, worm, lung, womb, feet, sore, legs, stye, jaws, or rump. Many of these, you will notice, have the important qualification as obscenities of coming from below the belt.

The more conservative porsenographer, however, need not be deprived of his old repertoire of dirty words. All he will have to do is to resort to rhyming slang, and use a new lot of code-words for old favourites, such as fibre (glass), Donald (Duck), Derry's (walls), Holman (Hunt), Exchange (and Mart), station (clock), please-be- (quick), Bath (chap) and bridle (and bit).

99

But this is all unfortunately in the future. Until then we are stuck with the devalued currency of the old vocabulary of words no longer worth the newsprint they're always being printed on. Our only hope is to turn to our fellow members in the Common Market, and borrow from a brand-new stock of swear-words which can be imported free of duty and VAT, and show what good Europeans we are.

The French, Germans and Italians can supply us with a vocabulary of colourful oaths and insults ranging from the mild, suitable for senior citizens, to the obscene, suitable for children – who, as we know, may be obscene but not absurd.

Many of these words, of course, should remain in their original form. To translate a word like *merde* from the French merely lands us up with a commonplace, and no longer effective English four-letter word. Properly pronounced, either with the gutteral 'r' of 'received' French, or with the rolled 'r' of the Midi, *merde* can be an expressive word and bring great relief to the feelings of those who utter it.

It is the simpler French exclamations, however, which can bring a novel charm to our invective when translated literally.

My source of the collection of French phrases that follows is my sister Angela, who has been married to two Frenchmen in her time and so has learnt what she's talking about the hard way, and her daughter Natalie, who was born in France and has worked in the theatre, and is therefore as well practised as her mother in the art of the French language of the most coarse.

In addition to the literal English translations for use in this country, I have included the original French words for those who would like to show off both here and in France.

Name of a pipe!	*Nom d'une pipe!*
Name of a dog!	*Nom d'un chien!*
Sky!	*Ciel!*
Go cook an egg!	*Va te faire cuire un œuf!*
Go and get seen!	*Va te faire voir!*
Leave the camp!	*Fous le camp!*

(Note: *Fous le camp!* comes from *foutre* – described by my two *collaboratrices* as 'a v. rude verb'. The dictionary says it is 'exceedingly fam. for' the verb *ficher*, which means to drive in, thrust in. It is also fam. for the French verbs *donner*, *mettre*, *faire* and *dire*. Used as an interjection *Foutre!* is not at all polite in French, but well worth using for its explosive sound in England. The euphemism is *Fichtre*, and rather tame, I think.)

God's brothel!	*Bordel de Dieu!*
By blue!	*Parbleu!*
Holy blue!	*Sacre bleu!*
Good blood!	*Bon sang!*
Thunder of God!	*Tonnerre de Dieu!*
A thousand thunders!	*Mille tonnerres!*
Semen of my ancestors!	*Semence de mes aïeuls!*

Further French exclamations worth using in their own right and permissible in France are *Flûte!* as a variant of *Zut!*, *sapristi!* and *saperlepopette* or *saperlotte* meaning Damnation! or Good God! and euphemisms for *sacristi*.

French insults do not translate particularly well. Again, like some of the exclamations, it is worth saying them in their original language, where they have both richness and acidity.

Only four of the insulting nouns my family collected for me bear translation, largely on the grounds of quaintness of idiom. They are all – Women's Libertines will be pained to hear – insults to women. The French will describe a slut as a crane *(grue)* or carrion *(charogne)*, a bitch as a bitch *(chienne)*, an old bitch as an old goat *(vielle bique)* and a whore as a trainee.

At least, the French is *traînée*, meaning a woman who is dragged along, and it seems a pity not to use a familiar and respectable English word to provide a convenient equivalent.

A little unfairly perhaps, a great many insults which apply only to men are feminine nouns. Regardless of which rates as the feminine partner of a pair of consenting male adults, the French would use the term *une lope*.

Crapule (f) and *fripouille* (f) are another couple of rich-sounding feminine nouns for hurling at a debauched, disgusting, low and blackguardly man whose behaviour is that of a *dégueulasse*. He can also be branded as *tête de cochon,* or pig's head ('pig-headed' is plain *stupide*).

Finally, there is a choice selection of insults suitable for use when spoken in French in England but which, although quite a few of them appear in respectable dictionaries, are probably best avoided in France, except by those who believe it's time the entente was finally de-cordialized anyway. (Experience has taught me that abroad English invective is more effective when abusing greedy taxi drivers, porters or importunate pedlars. In their language anything you can swear they can swear better. Keep to your traditional old-world native repertoire and you will not only relieve your own feelings more naturally, but certainly by your tone of voice, impress your adversaries that you mean business.)

The choice selection for me by my sister and niece was subtitled 'very rude and (. . .)'.

Starting with the (. . .) we have *con* (m), *conasse* (f), *connard* (m), all of which are unlikely dysphemisms – as, indeed, they are in English – for stupidity. There is also the noun *emmerdeur* (*emmerdeuse* f), derived from *merde,* and meaning a bore. This is obviously a word with a great future in élitist criticism: 'The *œuvre* of Jean-Jacques Connard is that of an inspired *emmerdeur* . . .'

The rest of the selection includes some satisfying expressions such as *garce* for bitch or strumpet, and *catin*, which means the same, with harlot as an optional extra. *Catin* is also the French equivalent of Kate, which seems an unnecessary aspersion to cast on many poor innocent girls. But then, as we know, Jane in English can be used in the same way and be equally disreputable, when people remember that it originally came from Jane Shore, the rhyming slang for what Cockneys, being entirely unable to sound a final 'r' in the right place, would call a haw.

People who live in Shropshire should feel at home with

at least one pop., fam., and vulg. French epithet, and that is *salop*, which is the basis of variants such as *salaud*, *saligaud*, *salopard*, all meaning a 'dirty fellow'. Men, however, escape comparatively lightly. A woman who is a *salope*, *salaude*, or *saligaude* can be a sloven, slattern, slut, drab, mopsey, trollop, wench, bitch or harlot.

Personally, if I must call a woman any of these names I think I would prefer *pouffriasse*. There's something cosier about it, somehow.

It is, as they say, 'arguable' that German is the ugliest of the principal languages of Europe (other ugly Germanic languages such as Dutch and Scandinavian aren't really principal enough to count), but for that very reason its uneuphoniousness makes it a suitable language for swearing in. Euphony has no place in rough Coarse Language.

One of the most remarkable features of German oaths and invective is that the mountains of guttural splutteral ferocity of the actual sound produced should give birth to such mini-mice of ideas.

However, with no good swear-words left in the English language, beggars can't be choosers. We have to replace our lost heritage somehow from somewhere.

The list below gives the original German oaths followed by the anti-climax of the English translation to be incorporated into our new vocabulary.

Donnerwetter!	Thunder-weather!
Donnerundblitzen!	Thunder and lightning!
Verdammter Schweinhund!	Damned pig-dog!
Verfluchter Schweinhund!	Cursed swine-hound!
Rabenaas!	Raven-vulture! (scoundrel)
Teufelsbraten!	Devil's roast! (scoundrel)
Miststück!	Dung piece! (bastard)

Brechsau!	Break-sow! (bastard)
Hurensohn!	Trollopson!
Vögler!	Fowler!
So eine Vögelei!	Such a birdery!

The verb *vögeln* and the noun *Vögelei* are v. rude, even (...) slang terms, best used in their literal, not figurative, sense in English.

Finally, and my favourite of all, there is the famous oath in Goethe's play *Goetz von Berlichingen,* which in German reads: '*Himmel, Arsch und Zwirn!*' Translated into moderate English as 'Heaven, bottom and linen thread' it should enrich our repertoire no end, and make a worthy successor to the obsolete 'Hell's bells and buckets of blood!'

Italian, as you might expect, has a picturesque vocabulary of oaths and invective, with a repertoire of obscenities and

bawdy plots dating back to Roman times and greatly relished by Chaucer and Boccaccio.

The milder forms of interjection and abuse translate neatly into English, and can be used in the original language in general Italian company.

Accidenti!	
Accipicchi!	Accidents!
Acciderba!	
Capperi!	Capers! [edible sort]
Porca miseria!	Dirty misery!
Mamma mia!	Mummy mine!
Crepa!	Burst!
Scoppia!	Burst!

The next grade is what my adviser on the rougher Coarse Italian calls 'medium'. From his personal repertoire I have selected these terms of personal abuse:

Testa di cavolo!	Head of cabbage!
Cornuto!	Cuckold! (a more serious term in Italy than here)

A third phrase, an abbreviation of *un uomo tre volte buono* can be translated three ways by carefully consulting the dictionary:

Buono tre volte!	Good three times!
	Good three volts!
	Good three vaults!

Whichever English version you may choose, to the Italian the term means a simpleton – or as we might say, a mentally retarded bloody fool.

Lastly, the blasphemous and obscene, which are best said in Italian. To translate them would, as with *merde,* merely be to repeat in English what has been current for centuries and land us back in the old and now ineffectual vocabulary we are trying to replace.

The following abusive obscenities are recommended for situations of frustration, pain and anger, as for instance when somebody treads on your toes.

When the offender is a man: *Testa di cazzo!*
                               Coglione!
                               Bucaiolo!
                               Culaio!
                               Culattiere!
                               Culattino!
When the offender is a woman: *Puttana!*

From *puttana* the equivalent of son of a bitch is easily formed as *figlio di puttana,* to be directed at the male offender; but it should be remembered that in Tuscany it is regarded as a mild and rather affectionate expression. However, I daresay it will mean what you want it to in Soho.*

It is advisable to be careful with the three words *culaio, culattiere,* and *culattino.* You must not, I mean, go into an Italian grocer's and ask for 300 grams of *culattino* when you want *culatello,* which is a rump of pork cured like ham and very good indeed. Nor must you ask for *culattiere* when you need *culatta,* which you get at the butcher and is the extreme top back of round of beef.

Food also stretches another trip-wire for the unwary, who are always in danger of confusing *fico,* which means a fig, and *fica,* which doesn't. In the dictionaries *fica* is defined as '(vulg.) female pudenda'. It can serve as a satisfactory exclamation for use in situations of frustration,

---

* The same sort of disarming thing happens in Sussex, where local custom raises an eyebrow or two by using the word 'fornicate' to mean, not what you mean, but what they mean – which is to dawdle and waste time and not make up one's mind. It is common usage to say of a dithering customer, 'He does fornicate so!'

pain and anger, as for instance, when you stub your own toes.

One suitable phrase for such an occasion is *porco fottuto!* This comes from the verb *fottere*, the Italian counterpart of the 'v. rude verb' *foutre* of the French mentioned earlier in this chapter.

Used as adjectives *porco* and the feminine *porca* are very important in the practice of blasphemy. Although literally meaning 'dirty', they correspond more nearly to 'bloody'. The formula is simple: you use the adjective and follow it with the name of any sacred person – as *porca madonna*.

Modern life offers a wide choice of public, if not always sacred, figures to swear by – like *porco Brezhnev*, or *porca Signora Maria Casabianca*, or *porco Aroldo Wilson*. The choice is endless.

The careful student of porsenography will probably have noticed the scarcity of four-letter words in the languages I have drawn on. Only *fica* of the many 'v. rude and (. . .) words' listed has the statutory four letters. Foreigners generally seem to favour five letters or more, with the exception of one three-letter word used by the French.

What philological reason there is for this, I do not know. The four-letter monosyllable seems to be peculiarly Anglo-Saxon. Abroad, the use of four-letter words, indeed, seems almost entirely confined to harmless childish expressions like *pipi*, which is common to French, German, Italian and Spanish.

It's very odd and ought to be gone into. People have got degrees for writing papers on less worthy subjects before now.

12 *Last Words*

In the time I have spent writing this little handbook there has been no noticeable change in the general standard of spoken and written English – and this in spite of the growing awareness in obscurer corners of The Media that the question has become of national importance, and must be taken seriously if we are not to lose our language and end up by speaking like the moronic announcers and disc jockeys of Radio 1 and whatever type of baboon the commercial stations are intent on plaguing us with.

The staff of the Top People's Paper (we used to call it the Tuppenny Daily at one time) are still in the van, though some would say they should be in the tumbrel. No less than a first leader (I trust not by the Celtic editor) proclaimed 'As of now, Western Europe is much more heavily dependent than America on Arab supplies . . .' Another writer wrote 'The possibility . . . has exacerbated fears of an unmanageable position . . .'

Before at last being taken over again by a literate columnist in 1973, the gossip column signed PHS referred to some young women of whom 'none, thankfully, wore a Princess Anne cowboy scowl'. And in the same column: 'I asked the steward whether he had a fire-extinguisher.

The steward . . . said he did not.' Seems like the writer did ought to had done his grammar lessons more better, don't it?

Even when its staff leave the paper the new *Times* style of broken English follows them around. Mr Ian Trethowan left his job as a feature writer to become managing director of BBC Radio. In due course he made a public pronouncement. 'The BBC [local] stations,' he said, 'have shown that community broadcasting can add a new dimension to the spectrum of the communications media.'

In such days of dazzling prose as these that passage stands out as a masterpiece.

Not long after adding this new dimension to the spectrum of non-communication, Mr Trethowan announced his intention of improving the pronunciation of his newsreaders and announcers. I can't remember if there was actually going to be a Crash Programme to eliminate what he called pronunciation 'clangers', but we were confidently assured that things would be stricter from then on.

The managing director's intent was scarcely declared before the Corp., led by Radio 4, embarked on a Festival of the Mis-spoken Word with a sparkling display of the modern BBC's ignorance of when and where to stress nouns and verbs.

We were told that fares would be *in*creased (why not raised?) and that the move would *con*flict with Government policy.

But the choicest clangers came from those new-dimension-adjoiners and spectrum-structurers, the local stations.

One of them told us that after a strike of ships' officers, the 'Dover Balloon service' had been resumed – a welcome piece of news to all environmentalists after that noisy cross-channel hovercraft service. The same newsreader told us of plans for a new yacht 'mariner'. I suppose he meant 'marina'. Mariners are not unknown in yachting, so it was difficult to tell.

Then Radio Brighton distinguished itself by telling us of '*de*lays' caused by traffic jams. This was a really brand new one and couldn't be blamed on the unfortunate Americans. And yet it had an undeniable idiot logic about it. If an *in*crease of the number of cars de*lays* traffic, then traffic *de*lays must surely in*crease* congestion.

But the gem of the Festival came from one of Mr Trethowan's announcerettes on Radio London. She told her listeners she would 'forward their letters back'.

I've never stayed up late enough to hear Radio London close down, but I'm sure their version of the National Anthem ends with

> Forward her victorious,
> Fab., and euphorious,
> Hopefully, the time-scale of her viability will be
>   open-ended,
> God maintain our Queen conservationwise.

And with those loyal thoughts, let us end with the hope that while he's saving the Queen, God will not be too busy to forward as much assistance as possible to the Queen's English in its struggle for survival.

Heaven knows it needs it.

Ringmer,
Sussex